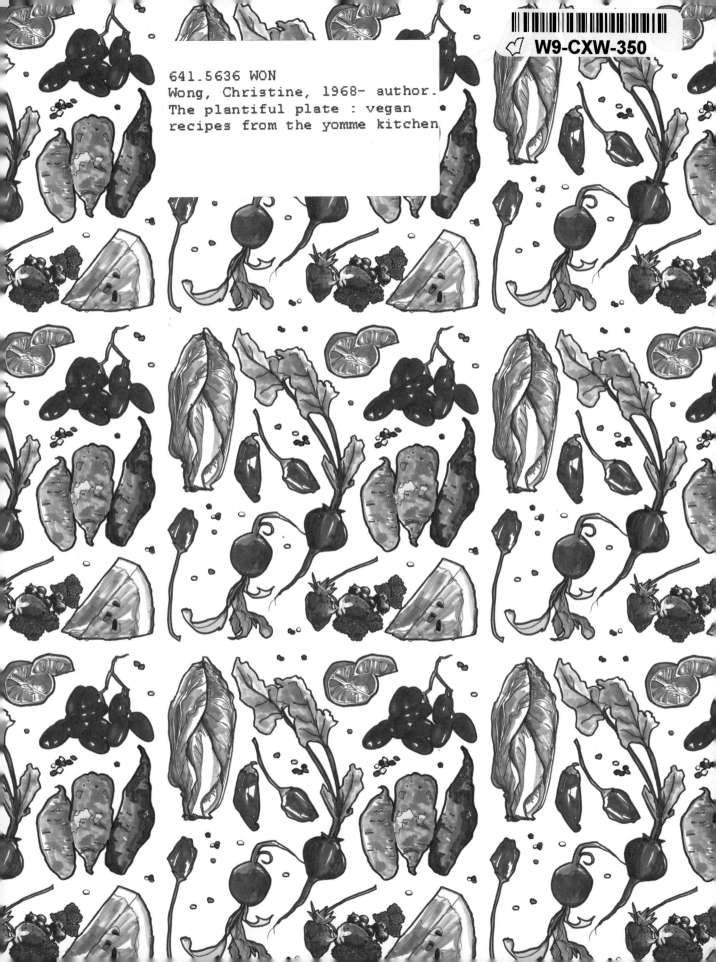

THE PLANTIFUL PLATE

Ratatouille's Ratatouille, page 187

THE PLANTIFUL PLATE

VEGAN RECIPES from THE YOMMME KITCHEN

CHRISTINE WONG

Fountaindale Public Library
Bolingbrook, IL
(630) 759-2102

THE COUNTRYMAN PRESS
A division of W. W. Norton & Company
Independent Publishers Since 1923

For information about permission to reproduce selections from this book, write to
Permissions, The Countryman Press, 500 Fifth Avenue, New York, NY 10110

For information about special discounts for bulk purchases, please contact
W. W. Norton Special Sales at specialsales@wwnorton.com or 800-233-4830

Manufacturing through Asia Pacific Offset
Book design by Endpaper Studio
Production manager: Devon Zahn
Illustrations: Michael Ward
Portrait photos: Monica Wong, Abbey Corbett

Instagram feature photos: Joscelyn Abreu, Mireille Azar, Susanna Bingemer, Kerstin Brachvogel,
Nate Burrows, Kimberly Espinel, Verena Frei, Gudrun Gerzabek, Amisha Gurbani, Olena Hassell,
Jutri Herman, Jessica Hoffman, Zuliya Khawaja, Meera Nalavadi, Ika Putri Novitawati, Nancy
Partington, Sebastian Perez, Sara Kiyo Popowa, Monisha Sharma, Sheil Shukla, Reethika Singh,
Rachel Steenland, Didi van Haren, Nisha Vora, Aviva Wittenberg, and Dora Xindaras

Names: Wong, Christine, author.
Title: The plantiful plate : vegan recipes from the yomme kitchen / Christine Wong.
Description: New York, NY : Countryman Press, a division of W.W Norton &
Company Independent Publishers Since 1923, [2019] | Includes index.
Identifiers: LCCN 2018036648 | ISBN 9781682682678 (hardcover)
Subjects: LCSH: Vegan cooking. | Vegan cooking--Recipes. | Veganism. | LCGFT: Cookbooks.
Classification: LCC TX837 .W 2019 | DDC 641.⅝₃₆—dc23
LC record available at https://lccn.loc.gov/2018036648

The Countryman Press
www.countrymanpress.com

A division of W. W. Norton & Company, Inc.
500 Fifth Avenue, New York, NY 10110
www.wwnorton.com

978-1-68268-267-8

10 9 8 7 6 5 4 3 2 1

For future generations, may you discover and enjoy the earth's bounty and protect all the magic of the ocean

CONTENTS

INTRODUCTION

The Yommme® Kitchen is for people who want to incorporate more vegetables into their meals, whether they're beginners in the kitchen or they tend to make the same things again and again. Many people are intimidated by veggies because they don't know how to make them satisfying, fun, and exciting. This book will help make you more confident in the kitchen as you gain flexibility in creating foods and let go of any stress or fears you have about cooking.

Yommme is a name I created to encompass mindful cooking + delicious food + feeling great. As with yoga, the more you practice, the less you have to put effort into your practice—and the stronger you become.

Although I live in New York City, where home cooking is an anomaly, we eat at home 95 percent of the time because it's healthier, tastier, and more affordable, and doing so greatly reduces our carbon footprint. For the most part, I tend to use ingredients that are accessible and recognizable, which includes a lot of fresh and local produce.

As a self-taught cook, I have learned to think outside the "norm" by creating healthier versions of traditional favorites. I find inspiration almost everywhere—from discoveries of in-season produce at the local greenmarkets to experiences with people, places, and the sights around me, and even the occasional movie. One of my most popular dishes, Ratatouille's Ratatouille (page 187), has been featured on numerous reputable food-related social-media pages, and it's been re-created around the world by my friends and Instagram followers. It was inspired by the Pixar movie *Ratatouille*; the film's catchphrase, "Everyone can cook," is something I strongly believe in and advocate.

This book is a collection of recipes that I use all the time, provided in a format of versatile combinations I like to call "food vinyasas." They inspire the creation of hundreds of flavorful dishes. My approach centers around eating natural, plant-based foods and using whole ingredients, that is suitable for any lifestyle. The vinyasas are designed to allow for flexibility and creativity. This method of cooking helps reduce the fear of cooking, curbs reliance on processed foods by making conscious food choices, and builds the foundation for a lifetime of good eating.

My Story

As a health coach, I've made it my mission to inspire others to add more plant-based, and plastic-free, meals into their lives. I share my recipes and ideas to enable anyone, with any level of cooking experience and on any budget, to cook more consciously. Let's face it, it can be hard to choose to eat "healthy" when so many options may

REAL FOOD IS . . .

▸ Fresh, seasonal, local, and/or organic: This type of produce is not genetically modified or sprayed heavily with pesticides or gases to ripen during shipment.

▸ A whole ingredient: Whole ingredients include nuts, fruits, legumes, and vegetables. Fresh, local, or organic is preferable.

▸ Anything without a nutrition label: If a food does have a nutrition label, it should be minimally processed and include five or fewer ingredients. You should be able to recognize all the words in the ingredient list.

▸ Naturally sweet: Sweeteners should be 100 percent natural—for example, maple syrup and dates.

▸ Preferably not packaged in plastic.

seem more appealing, cheaper, and more convenient—but often also more harmful and wasteful.

Eating habits can become ingrained at a very early age, and the science shows our taste buds and brains can become addicted to the pleasurable reward of foods high in calories, sugar, and unhealthy fats. I admit to a lifelong penchant for constantly snacking on all kinds of crunchy, savory snacks.

It took me some time to realize the harmful effects of this habit, and I'm glad I've now found my way to plant-based, healthy snacking and eating. My meals are now a daily celebration of the versatility of vegetables and fruits. After all, you can juice them, steam them, or eat them raw; stew, roast, or grill them; and even fry them. Through this book, I hope to illustrate how easy and rewarding it can be to eat this way.

My earliest cooking memories are of my mother, who went to great lengths to cook all the recipes she saw in the *New York Times* "Best Recipes" column. Although I've never made them myself, my favorites were her salmon and broccoli soufflé and an herb and onion bread that inspired the flavors of my Essential Loaf recipe (page 75).

I began to "cook" on my own when I was 9 years old. We had a tiny strawberry patch in our backyard, and I made my own jam by squishing the berries in a plastic sandwich bag. We moved to Hong Kong when I was 12, and taking cues from my mother's love for entertaining and sharing food, I often brought large salads and bags of popcorn to share with friends at school.

I returned to the United States for college, attending Parsons School of Design in New York City to study graphic design. There, I often cooked in my dorm kitchen; even then, I understood that the rice and fresh vegetables I'd pick up in Chinatown were infinitely healthier for me than the fast-food options surrounding me—or my roommate's tins of Spam. After college, while living in Hong Kong and Tokyo, I gradually taught myself how to cook with the basics and discovered the joy of creating foods beyond the usual salads and popcorn for others to enjoy.

From finishing puzzles as a child to designing corporate identity programs in my work as a designer, I have always loved the process of creating something from start to finish. Now I experience that same joy through cooking. It's the same feeling whether I have a very specific dish in mind from the beginning or instead opening the refrigerator, taking stock of its contents, and improvising something.

In 2002, I moved back to New York City, this time with a husband and a brand-new baby. With an infant to feed, I became very focused on the quality of the ingredients in the foods I purchased and prepared. I wanted to provide the best nourishment possible for my family, which eventually included a second child. Shelf-stable baby foods were never an option because I couldn't bear to eat them myself, so I made my own purees using produce my husband and I regularly ate. I froze individual-ingredient purees in ice-cube trays and then made mix-and-match meals for my children, keeping the focus on diversity. I've continued this method of preparing food all the way through to today: I make time for meal-prep sessions every weekend to prepare different components for meals to serve during the week. With these components on hand, it's easy to build a meal during busy weekdays. That's how many Asian restaurants are able to create such extensive menus!

I'm always mixing things up with my home cooking and getting my children involved in the kitchen. Most nights, we sit down together for dinner as a family. We like to eat family style, with such a variety of dishes that there's something for everyone, as well as room to try new foods. As a result, my kids are great eaters—and adventurous ones, too!

In 2007, I started my blog, www.c-cooking.com, to share with my community of mommy friends who were struggling with trying to get their children to eat anything other than chicken fingers. There, I shared basic, made-from-scratch recipes and received great feedback from an increasing audience.

After I'd been blogging for a few years, I wanted to ensure that the information I was providing was actually healthy, so I enrolled in a yearlong program at the Institute of Integrative Nutrition in 2013. This self-guided course was a good starting platform that opened my eyes to the knowledge that the right foods can heal and that some convenience or factory-made foods can cause great harm. From there, my own journey into a plant-strong diet began, and I haven't looked back.

The changes in my eating habits—focusing on whole ingredient "real" foods, and cutting out white flour and sugar, meat, and dairy—put an end to my vertigo, muscle cramps, and skin problems. My energy levels are high, and my memory is sharp. I always thought it was a myth, but "brain fog" is a very real condition. If I hadn't taken the steps to clean up my meals, I never would have recognized it.

I generally try to create dishes that are vegan, gluten-free, and low in sodium, and use natural sugars. Homemade foods have none of the stabilizers and hidden ingredients found in packaged and prepared foods, and everyone in my family feels better. I believe that if you're conscious about what you eat more than 90 percent of the time, there's no need to be super strict and avoid all the foods that are available on special occasions or when dining out.

I make all the meals and dishes you'll find in these pages in my tiny (8'7" × 8'8") NYC kitchen and usually have to shift things around often to get to the tools I need. Being Chinese, I tend to prefer Asian flavors; my English husband prefers a more Western palate, so our meals vary from dumplings to ratatouille to curries throughout the week. We love to "eat the world"—really.

This collection of recipes includes a lot of my personal favorites that I've adapted into clean, healthy, plant-based versions of packaged products or foods served in Chinese restaurants. I've seen lasting improvements in the general health of my family as a result of changing how we eat at home: our moods are better, we have more energy, and we rarely get sick.

As I've continued to grow my business during the past five years, I started leading cooking workshops and developed an online 10-day diet-reboot program that focuses on real, whole ingredient foods. The participants—both in person and virtually—are always impressed by how easy it can be to put together healthy and delicious food. At the same time, they're able to kick their cravings for addictive foods, like sugars, carbs, and meat. It means so much to me that I am able to effectively influence these positive changes and to help people learn that cooking can be fun, creative, and inspired—and that it can help them feel great!

Why Embrace Plant-Strong and Waste-Free Living?

Food isn't just fuel. It can also harm your body if you're constantly eating stuff it just can't handle. Depending on the individual, symptoms of a poor diet can include fatigue, skin issues, aches and pains, and chronic illnesses. Since I've made changes to my own diet, I've become a strong supporter of bringing vegetables to the forefront of daily meals in a practical and tasty way.

I developed the Yommme philosophy when working with my clients and members of my diet-reboot program. Its focus is on the principles of balancing and nourishing life with food prepared from flexible recipes. Eating more plant-based foods is a lifelong habit that we need to embrace as a society for the benefit of our own health, as well as for the health of the planet.

Just as we exercise our bodies daily, we need to be mindful of what we eat to nourish and strengthen both body and mind. The more conscious you become as you purchase, prepare, and eat food, the easier it becomes to eat cleanly and be less wasteful.

IN-SEASON PRODUCE

SPRING	SUMMER	AUTUMN	WINTER
Asparagus	Basil	Artichoke	Beets
Chives	Beans	Beans	Bok choy
Garlic scapes	Beets	Beets	Brussels sprouts
Herbs	Celery	Broccoli	Butternut squash
Lettuce	Chard	Brussels sprouts	Cabbage
Peas	Collards	Cauliflower	Carrots
Scapes	Corn	Celery	Cauliflower
Snap peas	Cucumbers	Chard	Celeriac
Spinach	Eggplant	Chestnuts	Legumes
	Fennel	Chili peppers	Onions
Blood orange	Kale	Corn	Parsnips
Grapefruit	Lettuce	Cranberry beans	Potatoes
Kumquats	Mint	Edamame	Pumpkin
Rhubarb	Okra	Fennel	Radishes
Strawberries	Peppers	Ginger	Romanesco
	Squash blossoms	Kale	Rosemary
	Tomatillos	Kohlrabi	Rutabaga
	Tomatoes	Leeks	Shiitake mushrooms
	Zucchini	Lettuce	Sunchokes
		Mushrooms	Turnips
	Avocado	Okra	
	Blueberries	Onions	Apples
	Cantaloupe	Parsnips	Cranberries
	Cherries	Peppers	Oranges
	Currants	Potatoes	Pears
	Figs	Pumpkin	Persimmon
	Husk cherries	Shishito	Pomegranate
	Mango	Spinach	
	Peaches/nectarines	Sweet potatoes	Chestnuts
	Pineapple	Tomatillos	Pulses
	Raspberries	Tomatoes	
	Watermelon	Turmeric	
		Turnips	
		Zucchini	
		Apples	
		Blackberries	
		Grapes	
		Pears	
		Plums	
		Quince	

You can make conscious choices every step of the way, from food shopping to using food scraps in soups or stocks or sending them back to the earth via composting. All these little things make a difference toward a fulfilling life that is less cluttered and more efficient.

Whether it's advertising, colorful packaging, cost-efficient pricing, or chemically enhanced fast-food triggers that draw you in, it's easy to become enticed by and addicted to factory-made pseudofoods. It's tough for a simple vegetable to compete against a flavorful product designed in a lab to push all the right satisfaction buttons. This is the main reason why so many kids aren't interested in real food. It's disheartening to know that children are developing chronic, adult-onset diseases as a result of this eating mindset.

I believe in being proactive, rather than reactive. By building and maintaining a strong and conscientious nutritional foundation, you can stay healthier and maybe even avoid getting sick in the first place. A kitchen full of colorful fruits and vegetables has a lot more appeal than a cabinet full of colorful medicines! I'm not saying that you'll never need a doctor if you eat clean, but healthy eating is an excellent foundation for good health.

Going Plastic-Free

The documentary *A Plastic Ocean* made me hyperaware of how much plastic has infiltrated our daily lives. It takes 450 years for plastic to break down, and even then, it never goes away. It ends up polluting the oceans, accumulating in oceanic currents called gyres; one is currently the size of Texas. Plastic has negatively impacted almost 700 species, including 60 percent of all sea birds and 100 percent of sea turtles, who mistake plastics for food. It's also coming back into our own food chain, as microplastics have been found in seafood, sea salt, and even tap-water samples around the globe.

The amount of plastics people use each day is alarming. Every person on the planet goes through 300 pounds of single-use plastic per year, 20 percent of which—that's more than 8 million tons of plastic—is dumped into the oceans each year. In fact, 50 percent of all plastics have an average usage span of 12 minutes; this includes the 2 million plastic bags used each minute around the world. All these single-use, "disposable" items are still going to be around for centuries, and they will keep building up unless we collectively make a change in our buying habits. A continuous accumulation of bags, water bottles, straws, takeout containers, cutlery, toothbrushes, pens, and countless other items is simply unsustainable.

When I shop for groceries, I always bring my own bags (a carrier, as well as produce bags) and containers to avoid taking any of these single-use plastic items. Once, I purchased handmade noodles from a restaurant in my own container, thus avoiding the waste of three styrofoam containers, a plastic bag, and the utensils they always throw in . . . that's almost 10 items in one simple takeout order!

Being plastic-free requires shopping around the perimeter of supermarkets and eating fresh fruits and vegetables. Farmers' markets and ethnic markets are good places to find fresh, unpackaged produce. I always rinse my produce, so there really isn't a need to keep each produce item in separate bags.

Eating in season is also key, so no strawberries in February—unless I've saved some from summer in the freezer. Your body adjusts to the climate better when you eat foods that are locally grown and readily available. For example, root vegetables will ground you and keep you warmer in the winter than coconut–pineapple smoothies.

I've always been an advocate of using glass and stainless steel containers for everything from my children's baby bottles and lunch containers to my own water bottle and food-storage containers. Everything just tastes better without plastic touching it. Recently, BPAs were singled out as being harmful, but who's to say that other components of plastics used in food packaging won't be considered unsafe in the future? Manufacturers are not required to disclose what their packaging is made of. And what's cheap and convenient for producers doesn't necessarily translate to good health.

Plastic-free living is not just a lifestyle choice intended to save the environment. The chemicals used to create plastics leach into foods. They have the power to disrupt the endocrine system, releasing estrogen-like chemicals. Even after converting to a healthy, plant-strong diet, I still wasn't feeling right, suffering from a constant pain on the left side of my body for an entire year and extremely irregular monthly cycles. I saw numerous doctors and specialists, but none could explain what was happening to me; all I learned was that I was nowhere near being menopausal. I didn't pursue medical treatment for the unknown cause of my health woes, but ever since I stopped eating foods packaged in single-use plastic,

including salad leaves, coconut milk, frozen fruits, and a few snack items, everything has returned to normal.

Storing food in plastic is also a source of food waste. Breathable materials are better, as they prevent moisture from getting trapped and developing mold. Plastic toxins leach out more aggressively into oily, acidic foods and foods that are hot. The lids of some glass jars have a plastic lining, so it's best to make sure foods never touch the lining and that it has cooled to room temperature before closing the jar, so condensation doesn't allow contaminates from the plastic to leach into the food. When blending hot foods, such as soups, use an immersion stick blender or glass blender; if your appliances are plastic, let the food cool completely before you blend it. Of course, we now know to never heat foods in the microwave in plastic containers.

Always take stock of what you own, and use it regularly. Unless your utensils are damaged, it's not necessary to replace them. However, if your cutting boards, nonstick pans, and cooking tools have nicks and cuts, you should replace them to keep plastics out of your food.

The recipes in this book use ingredients that are free of single-use plastic packaging. While it's hard to avoid plastics altogether, as refrigerators are lined with plastic and kitchen appliances and bulk-food bins are often made of plastic, you can still consciously choose to avoid plastics by storing your food in glass or stainless steel containers and never buying foods packaged in plastic. For example, after I learned that sea salt around the world is contaminated by plastic pollution, I switched to kosher salt.

In November 2017, I reached out to friends in the Instagram food community to create a charity project to protect the oceans. My #plasticfreefoodie emagazine (vol. 1) launched with a collection of 80 recipes contributed by more than 60 inspirational food Instagrammers and zero-waste influencers. The contributors, based in Australia, New York, Germany, India, and points in between, shared with their collective 5.5 million followers an important message beyond the beautiful foods they create and showcase each day. Following the magazine's release, in January 2018, I launched a 30-day #plasticdetox challenge on my social media channels to raise plastic usage awareness. My goal is to share the reasons why we need to change our spending habits and how we can achieve this. I hope this book conveys the same message.

Buying in Bulk

The bulk-food sections of supermarkets are a convenient place to find dry-good pantry items. I save all the glass jars from the condiments we use, so I have a variety of shapes and sizes to fill with these bulk items as we need them. While New York City has a great recycling program, my personal preference is to refuse and reduce waste. Knowing that I don't accumulate new bottles for pantry staples each time I buy them is hugely satisfying.

To determine how much of a bulk-food item you're buying, you must first weigh the empty jar to find out its decimal weight (its *tare*). Upon checkout, this number is deducted from the filled weight of the jar. To avoid having to do this each time, it's a good idea to write the jar's empty weight on its lid or side, or to keep a handy list of the tare numbers and bulk-food item numbers (*PLUs*) or prices per pound for the places where you shop. My list is on my phone.

I've reassessed and replaced all the packaged-in-plastic food items I used to have in my pantry. In New York City, Whole Foods Market offers a good selection; I've also joined a member-run food co-op that has an extensive array of bulk foods and more (see the table below). I visit the co-op each week with a bag full of miscellaneous jars and a list (always have a list!) and stock up on everything from nuts and flours to olive oil and miso paste to spices and dish soap. I can even buy nori seaweed by the sheet! It's a great way to buy only what you need and to prevent waste. I also take photos of the empty jars on the scale to show the cashier and to avoid any confusion.

Bulk-item foods can usually be found in natural food stores. Check out www.litterless.com/wheretoshop for an extensive list of North American locations. Another way to avoid waste is to purchase a 25- or 50-pound bag of a dry-good pantry item you use often. You can use it yourself all year long or share it with friends and family.

Eating Plants

Veganism is a lifestyle that promotes a more humane and caring world. The sad state of meat production today is enough to make anyone consider eating less meat and animal byproducts, including dairy and eggs. As plastics in the oceans are ingested by marine life, plastic particles end up embedded in seafood; one study revealed that seafood eaters ingest up to 11,000 microplastics each year. We're simply too far removed from our food sources. It's time to take charge and know exactly what you're putting into your body.

Adopting a healthy, vegan diet means eating vegetables . . . lots of them, as well as including protein in balanced meals. I personally

BULK-FOOD ITEMS

LEGUMES

Adzuki/Aduki beans
Black beans
Black-eyed peas
Chickpeas (garbanzo beans)
Jacob's cattle beans
Kidney (red) beans
Lentils, French
Lentils, green
Lentils, red
Lima (baby white) beans
Mung beans
Navy (white) beans
Peas, green, split
Peas, yellow, split
Pinto beans
Soybeans (organic)

FLOUR

All-purpose flour, whole wheat
Bread flour, whole wheat
Brown rice flour (gluten-free)
Buckwheat flour
Cornmeal, coarse (polenta)
Cornmeal, medium
Pastry flour, whole wheat
Rye flour
Spelt flour, whole grain

GRAINS

Amaranth
Barley, hulled
Buckwheat, raw
Buckwheat, roasted (kasha)
Cracked wheat
Gluten-free oats, rolled
Grits
Kamut
Millet
Oat groats, steel cut
Oat groats, whole
Oats, rolled
Quinoa, red
Quinoa, white
Rye berries
Spelt berries
Teff
Wheat berries, hard red spring

NUTS & SEEDS

Almonds, raw, unpasteurized
Brazil nuts, raw
Cashews, curried
Cashews, raw, whole
Cashews, raw, pieces
Cashews, roasted, salted
Chia seeds, raw
Flax seeds, golden
Hemp seeds, hulled
Macadamia nuts
Peanuts, split
Pecans, raw

Pepitas (pumpkin seeds)
Pistachios, salted
Pistachios, unsalted
Sesame seeds, unhulled
Walnuts, raw

OIL, VINEGAR & SAUCES

Canola oil, expeller pressed
Coconut oil, raw
Olive oil, extra virgin
Sesame oil, toasted
Sunflower oil, high oleic
Tamari (wheat free)
Vinegar, rice

PASTA

Cous-cous, French
Cous-cous, whole wheat
Pasta, spirals brown rice
Penne, rigate, whole wheat
Penne, rigate, semolina
Soba
Spaghetti, brown rice
Udon

RICE

Basmati, brown
Basmati, white
Jasmine, brown
Long-grain, brown
Short-grain, brown
Red rice
Purple sticky rice
Sweet brown rice
Wild rice

SEA VEGETABLES

Dulse, flakes
Dulse, leaf
Laver, wild Atlantic nori
Nori sheets
Kombu

SWEETENERS

Brown rice syrup, genmai
Cane juice, evaporated (dry)
Honey, bulk
Maple syrup, grade A dark
Molasses, blackstrap
Sucanat (fair trade)

CHOCOLATE

Cacao nibs
Agave nectar, light, raw
Dark chocolate chips

DRIED FRUIT

Apple rings, dried
Apricots, dried

Cherries, Bing,
 sun-dried
Coconut, shredded
Cranberries, whole
Dates, Medjool
Dates, Arya, pitted
Figs, Black Mission
Figs, Turkish
Goji berries, sun-dried
Mango, dried
Pineapple, dried
Prunes, dried
Raisins, Thompson

SPICES

Alfalfa sprouting
 seeds
Allspice powder
Anise (star) pods
Arrowroot powder
Astragalus root slices
Barley grass powder
Basil, leaves
Basil holy (rama)
Bay leaf, whole
Bee pollen
Burdock root
Cacao powder, roasted
Calendula flowers
Caraway seeds
Cardamom pods
Cardamom powder
Carob powder
Cayenne powder
Chamomile flowers
Chili flakes
Chipotle powder
Cilantro leaves

Cinnamon (cassia)
 powder
Cinnamon (cassia) sticks
Clove powder
Clove, whole
Clover blossoms, red
Coriander, ground
Coriander seeds
Cumin powder
Cumin seeds
Curry powder
Dandelion roots
Dill weed
Dong quai root
Echinacea angustofolia
 root
Elderberries
Fennel seeds
Fenugreek seeds
Garam masala powder
Garlic granules
Ginger root powder
Ginko leaves
Herbs de Provence
 spice blend
Hibiscus flowers
Lavender flowers
Lemon balm
Lemongrass
Licorice root pieces
Maca root powder
Marjoram leaf
Mediterranean
 seasoning blend
Milk thistle seeds
Mullein leaves
Mustard seeds, brown
Nettle leaves
Nutmeg powder

Oatstraw
Onion granules
Oregano leaves
Paprika powder
Parsley leaves
Pepper, black, cracked
Peppercorns, black,
 whole
Peppermint leaf
Poppy seeds
Psyllium husk
Raspberry leaves
Reishi mushroom slices
Rosehips
Rosemary leaf
Rose petals, pink
Sage leaf
Sage, white ceremonial
Schisandra berries
Sea salt, smoked
Skullcap
Slippery elm bark
Spearmint leaves
Spirulina powder
St. John's Wort
Stevia leaf
Tarragon
Thyme leaf
Turmeric root powder
Vanilla beans, whole
Vitex berry powder
Witch hazel bark
Yarrow leaf and flowers

TEAS

Assam
Blossoms of Health
Chai (Oregon)
Darjeeling

Earl Grey
English breakfast
Hibiscus high blend
Honeybush
Kukicha twig
Oolong
Peace tea blend
Rooibos, green
Rooibos, red
Sencha green
Vita-blend
Yerba mate

MISCELLANEOUS

Baking powder
Baking soda
Coffee
Miso, brown rice
Miso, chickpea
Miso, sweet white
No-Meatballs (vegan)
Nutritional yeast
 (non-organic)
Popcorn
Sea salt, Hiwa Kai
 kosher
Sea salt, Bolivian rose
Sea salt, matcha
Sea salt, Celtic
Sea salt, fine
Sesame sticks
 (non-organic)
Tofu

know plenty of vegans and vegetarians who load up on sugary foods and starches and eat few or no vegetables. I'm not a dietician, but it's clear to me that this isn't a healthy, balanced option.

The top 12 plant-based protein sources are as follows, including the grams of protein they contain per serving:

Soybeans: 1 cup, cooked (28 grams)
Lentils: 1 cup, cooked (18 grams)
Black beans: 1 cup, cooked (15 grams)
Chickpeas: 1 cup, cooked (14 grams)
Hemp seeds: 2 tablespoons (10 grams)
Green peas: 1 cup, cooked (9 grams)
Quinoa: 1 cup, cooked (8 grams)
Almonds: ¼ cup (8 grams)
Almond butter: ⅛ cup (8 grams)
Rice + beans: 1 cup (7 grams)
Oatmeal: 1 cup, cooked (6 grams)
Spinach: 1 cup, cooked (5 grams)
Chia seeds: 2 tablespoons (4 grams)

How can you sustain a plant-based lifestyle? One of the methods below may be a good starting point in figuring out what's best for you.

▸ Take Mark Bittman's VB6 approach and eat clean (meaning gluten-free and vegan) each day until 6 p.m.
▸ Emphasize the vegetables in each meal. If you must incorporate some clean proteins and grains, serve them only as side portions.
▸ Eat clean on weekdays, and relax your rules on the weekends.
▸ Do a 10-day, 100 percent plant-powered, clean-eating detox once a month.

There's no right or wrong method. Choose whatever works best for you! But however you do it, remember: consistency is key! If you adopt a 90 percent plant-based life, or if you consider becoming a vegan, make sure you get plenty of iron-rich foods, including legumes, prune juice, spinach, lentils, edamame, pumpkin, and squash, and take a B12 vitamin.

Adopting a plant-based life and influencing others with your healthy lifestyle will make a difference. We could feed every human being on the planet if we avoided consuming meat and all adopted a plant-strong lifestyle.

Organic vs. Conventional

On one evening in the late '90s, before I knew anything about organic foods, I took the time to make a home-cooked meal for a dear friend. I clearly remember that even though I used fresh ingredients and seasoning, my meal was tasteless. I couldn't understand why, but a few years later, I came to understand how mass farming affects the quality and taste of produce. More recently, I've certainly found that to be true about avocados; as the world's demand for avocados increases, they just don't seem as flavorful as they used to. Then again, I do live in New York City—I'm sure they're much more delicious in California and Mexico!

Organic produce is more flavorful and safer to eat. Supporting organic growers with your dollars is worthwhile, but you'll find that some supermarkets differentiate organic produce by packaging it in plastic—somewhat contradicting the purpose of chemical-free products. Instead, shop at farmers' markets where vendors, for the most part, only use pesticides when necessary, and in small amounts. Many smaller farms cannot afford organic certification, even though their practices are organic. Speak to the people who work at farm stands to really get to know your food.

Organic can be pricier than conventionally grown produce, but they do have advantages, as I'll explain in the next two sections. Whatever is available to you, it is still always best to eat a variety of lots of fresh vegetables, than none at all.

Some fruits and vegetables absorb more pesticides than others. When possible, choose organic for these foods. See the 2017 Environmental Working Group's List of the Dirty Dozen in the box.

Buy what works for you and your budget. Eating healthy doesn't have to be expensive or complicated. Buying fresh, unpackaged whole foods is actually more cost effective than buying the prepared stuff.

"DIRTY" DOZEN

Strawberries	Grapes
Spinach	Celery
Nectarines	Tomatoes
Apples	Sweet bell
Peaches	peppers
Pears	Potatoes
Cherries	Hot peppers

"CLEAN" FIFTEEN

Sweet corn	Mangoes
Avocados	Eggplant
Pineapples	Honeydews
Cabbage	Kiwis
Onions	Cantaloupes
Sweet peas	Cauliflower
Papayas	Grapefruits
Asparagus	

Love the Uglies

All produce is not meant to be perfect and even in size and shape. I always love visiting the farmers' market and finding unique beauties. In the eyes of retailers, and according to standards of food uniformity, "ugly" produce often gets tossed out before consumers ever see them. One-third of the food produced every year in the world for human consumption—approximately 1.3 billion tons—ends up wasted. Even though they look a little different, "ugly" produce is perfectly nutritious and delicious. Looking less-than-perfect is 100 percent natural, but 40 to 50 percent of vegetables get tossed instead of being used to help the hungry and those who don't have access to or can't afford fresh foods.

In 2014, the French supermarket chain Intermarché launched a promotion called "Inglorious Fruits and Vegetables," marking down these "ugly" foods by 30 percent. Overall store traffic rose by 24 percent as customers hunted for grotesque apples, disfigured eggplants, failed lemons, ridiculous potatoes, hideous oranges, and more.

More recently, initiatives and organizations such as @uglyfruitandveg, @misfitjuicery, @imperfectproduce, and @hungryharvest, as well as my friends at @uglyproduceisbeautiful and @gothamgreens, celebrate and advocate the use of these beauties. Some market stands and supermarkets sell "aesthetically challenged" veggies at a fraction of the usual cost, making fresh produce more affordable. Here's a list of where you can find them around the globe: www.endfood waste.org/the-uf-v-supermarket-directory.html.

Eat Local

Not only is eating locally grown food better for the environment, as it involves the use of less fuel—it's also better for your health. Local produce is more flavorful and contains more nutrients, as it has fewer miles to travel. You're able to support your local economy and truly know more about your food—simply by talking to the source. Local food also supports the ayurvedic principle of eating only seasonal foods. Eating in-season fruits and vegetables helps keep your body in sync with the cycles of nature. Following are a few ways you can eat local:

▸ Community Supported Agriculture (CSA): In this model, a farm offers a certain number of "shares" to the public or its community. One share consists of a selection of seasonal vegetables. You can choose from a full share (weekly) or a half share (biweekly) for either a 22-week period or year-round, depending on the farm. Some CSAs offer other farm products, such as eggs, homemade breads, pastured meats, cheeses, fruits, or flowers. CSAs benefit farmers because they're paid in advance to grow a season's crops. Advantages for consumers:

    ▸ CSA produce is the freshest you can get, including all the flavor and vitamin benefits.

    ▸ You'll be introduced to new vegetables and new ways of cooking.

    ▸ You'll establish a relationship with the farmer and know more about the source of your food.

▸ To find a CSA near you, visit www.localharvest.org.

▸ Farmers' Markets/Farm Stands: If you can't nab a CSA share, local farmers' markets and farm stands offer a great selection of produce! To find farmers' markets near you, visit www.localharvest.org.

▸ Pick-Your-Own: Get the kids involved and visit a farm to pick your own produce! It's an adventure: a great day spent outdoors that's fun for everyone! At the end of the day, you'll probably come home with much more than you needed, but it's a great way to have your own "Iron Chef" moment, putting one ingredient to use in a lot of different recipes or preserving some for future use. To find farms that offer pick-your-own produce, visit www.pickyourown.org.

▸ Grow-Your-Own: Growing your own vegetables is a fun and an incredibly rewarding experience. Use flowerpots on a windowsill to grow a few herbs, or if you're lucky, you can farm your own little patch of land. The benefits are immeasurable: you'll reduce your environmental impact, save money, waste less food, and enjoy the accomplishment of nurturing your own nutrients—with no chemicals and processing. You can even grow food on your kitchen counter!

Sprouts

There's nothing like growing your own food and enjoying the nutritional benefits of eating fresh, live food. The best part: you can do it in the comfort of your own kitchen. You can find sprouting seeds in the bulk sections of some co-ops, but you can also order them online (for example, www.johnnyseeds.com/vegetables/sprouts). Make sure to ask them to send them without plastic packaging and not in a plastic-padded envelope.

1 tablespoon sprouting seeds (alfalfa, broccoli, clover, radish)
2 cups filtered water

1 quart mason jar
Cheesecloth for covering
String or rubber band for fastening

METHOD

Place the seeds in the mason jar and fill completely with the filtered water. Secure the string or rubber band around the neck of the jar. Set aside to soak overnight.

Drain the water from the seeds through the cheesecloth and invert the jar at a 45-degree angle resting in a medium-size bowl, positioned with access to airflow. Set this aside at room temperature and out of sunlight for 5 to 7 days, rinsing and draining the seeds twice daily.

When ready to harvest, pour the contents into a larger bowl. Fill with water and give it a good stir; the unsprouted seeds and hulls will float to the top. Skim these off and discard these into a compost bin. Drain the sprouts in a colander and set aside for 1 hour. Keep refrigerated in a jar.

Preparing Your Produce

Preparing your fruits and vegetables a few days in advance will help save time when you're ready to cook, and you'll always have a healthy snack available.

To naturally clean smaller produce like berries and grapes, combine 1 tablespoon (15 ml) of apple cider vinegar with 1 cup (240 ml) water in a bowl. Allow to sit for 5 minutes, stirring a couple of times for the vinegar to clean all surfaces. Remove and rinse very well. These are best cleaned right before eating.

For larger fruits and vegetables, like grapefruit and zucchini, use a spray bottle with the same vinegar-to-water ratio and spray completely before rinsing well. Allow them to air dry completely before storing.

Soaking Nuts and Seeds

Nuts are rich in unsaturated and omega-3 fats. Although these are healthy fats, nuts also are high in calories. Go easy on these if you're trying to lose weight. The right amount—about a handful (¼ cup) a day—can satisfy your appetite. Although nuts are a better choice than factory-made snacks, consuming too much nut fiber can lead to gastrointestinal problems.

Soaking nuts and seeds breaks down the phytic acid within them that binds to important minerals, making them less available for the body to digest. "Activating" them in filtered water and salt allows them to begin germinating, which breaks down the phytate and increases their digestibility and nutritional value. Drying them out afterward gives them back their crunch, but make sure they're completely dry!

To properly soak your nuts or seeds, cover them with plenty of filtered water. For 4 cups of nuts or seeds, add 1 tablespoon of salt to the soaking water.

Soaking time:

Almonds, hazelnuts, or pine nuts: 12 hours

Cashews or pistachios: 3 hours

Pecans or walnuts: 6 hours

Brazil or macadamia: 8 hours

Pumpkin, sesame, or sunflower seeds: 7 hours

METHOD

After soaking, rinse and drain the nuts or seeds. To dry them, place them on a tray in a sunny place or in the oven set at the lowest temperature for 12 to 24 hours, or until fully dry (if you have a dehydrator, set it at 100°F and dry them for 18 to 24 hours). Generally, it's easier to soak the seeds or nuts overnight, drain and discard the filtered water, and then spread them out on a baking sheet to dry out during the day. If you are planning to make a nut butter, the nuts must be thoroughly dry to prevent moisture and mold.

Soaking Grains

Soaking grains also increases the body's ability to digest them. As with nuts, this process neutralizes the phytic acid and also increases the content of beneficial enzymes and vitamins. Adding 1 teaspoon to 1 tablespoon of an acidic substance (for example, vinegar, kefir, or yogurt) to the soak makes the grains more digestible and also helps keep your blood sugar levels down.

For 1 cup of uncooked grains:

Amaranth / Buckwheat / Couscous / Millet / Oats / Quinoa / Rice
Filtered water (see chart below)
1 teaspoon to 1 tablespoon acidic substance (vinegar, kefir, or yogurt)

METHOD

Rinse well and drain. Cover with filtered water; add the acidic substance, if using; and set aside to soak for 7 to 24 hours.

Place the grains along with the soaking liquid in a small pot over high heat and bring to a boil.

Cover immediately with a tight-fitting lid, reduce the heat to low, and simmer until all the liquid is absorbed.

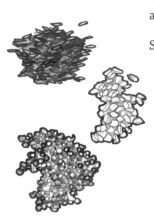

Soaking liquid quantity, cooking times, and cooked yield per 1 cup of grains:

Amaranth: 3 cups filtered water, 20 minutes, makes 3 cups
Buckwheat: 1½ cups filtered water, 10 minutes, makes 3 cups
Rice: 1½ cups filtered water, 20 to 30 minutes, makes 3 to 4 cups
Rolled oats: 2 cups filtered water, 5 minutes, makes 1½ cups
Steel-cut oats: 3 cups filtered water, 25 to 30 minutes, makes 4 cups
Millet: 2 cups filtered water, 10 minutes, makes 3½ cups
Quinoa: 2 cups filtered water, 10 minutes, makes 4 cups

Remove from the heat and set aside to rest for 5 to 10 minutes.

Fluff with a fork and serve immediately or set aside uncovered to cool to room temperature if using later. Transfer to an airtight container and refrigerate for future use.

A Note About Beans

Loaded with fiber, protein, iron, and B vitamins, legumes and beans are the perfect way to add more plant-based protein into your diet. Dried beans are an ideal food to stock in the pantry, but if they're old—perhaps sitting in your cupboard for 1 to 2 years—they can lose their nutrient content and won't soften, even with thorough cooking.

Making beans from scratch tastes so much better than cooking the canned kind! It really is worth a little effort. Cooking beans twice, or adding apple cider vinegar, bay leaves, garlic, fennel, kombu (dried seaweed), or cumin during cooking can aid in their digestion. Soak and cook a couple of different varieties at the same time, so they're convenient and ready to use for any recipe throughout the week.

Adzuki / black / borlotti / navy / pinto / red kidney / cannellini / or chickpeas
Filtered water, to cover
1 tablespoon baking soda or 2" piece of kombu

NOTE: Yellow, red, green, or French lentils don't need to be soaked before they're cooked.

METHOD

Rinse the beans well and sift through them, discarding any broken or discolored ones. Place each kind of bean in a separate bowl, cover with plenty of the filtered water, and add the baking soda or kombu to each bowl. Set aside to soak for 4 to 8 hours or overnight.

Drain and rinse well.

Place the different beans in separate saucepans and add enough water to cover the beans by 1 inch. Place over high heat and bring to a boil. Skim off and discard any foam that rises to the surface.

Reduce the heat to low and simmer at a low boil for 30 to 35 minutes.

Remove from the heat, drain well, and set aside to cool completely.

Transfer to an airtight container and refrigerate for future use (within 10 days).

AQUAFABA

If you are making chickpeas (1 part dried beans to 4 parts filtered water), you can make your own aquafaba. Just make sure not to add baking soda, and make certain there is no grease in the pot or on the utensils you are using. Soak and cook as directed above, but do not drain; instead, after removing from the heat, set aside to cool completely in the cooking liquid.

METHOD

Strain the chickpeas out, transfer the liquid to a second grease-free pot over high heat, and bring to a boil.

Reduce the heat to medium-low and simmer, uncovered, for 30 to 40 minutes, or until the liquid thickens and becomes slightly yellow. Remove from the heat and set aside to cool completely.

Transfer to an airtight container and refrigerate overnight. If you don't plan to use the chickpeas right away, add them to the aquafaba for the overnight chill.

The recipe for Aquafaba Whipped Cream can be found with the Raspberry Shortcake recipe (page 238).

THREE OF MY FAVORITE INGREDIENTS

Ginger: Fresh ginger stimulates appetite, aids digestion, and has powerful anti-inflammatory properties that help relieve nausea, muscle pain, migraines, and congestion. This medicinal root makes a great, warming, and natural tea: simply steep a 1-inch piece (either thinly sliced or grated) in boiled water for 5 to 10 minutes. Ginger tea is perfect in the fall and spring to help relieve seasonal allergies and in the winter to stimulate blood circulation and to fight off colds and flu.

Beets: The beet, which is among nature's most powerful antioxidants, is one of the healthiest vegetables you can consume. They're full of pure energy that aids in digestion, giving your entire body a revitalizing immunity boost. Beets are best eaten raw, either grated or thinly sliced into a salad or freshly pressed into your morning juice. Low in calories and full of fiber, they're a great food to support weight management. Beets give a brain or energy boost and are essential in cell detoxification and cleansing.

Dark, leafy greens: In my opinion, no meal is complete without a dose of dark, leafy greens, such as beet or radish greens, bok choy, chard, collards, kale, or spinach. Packed with fiber and nutrients like vitamins A, C, K, and folate, they help maintain healthy brain and body function. In terms of taste, they add depth to any smoothie or salad as well as freshness and a pop of color to any cooked meal.

Fermented Foods

Your intestines are the roots of your body, and feeding them fermented foods helps maintain and grow a healthy body ecosystem. Fermented foods are a good source of probiotics (gut-friendly bacteria), which improve digestion; boost the immune system; are high in B vitamins; help fight infections and anxiety; improve skin and energy levels; and energize the mind.

The recipes for Pickles (page 151), Kimchi (page 153), and Kombucha (page 88) are examples of age-old traditions of fermentation. Homemade versions are much better for you than ultra-pasteurized processed versions, which lose all their beneficial bacteria due to food-safety processes and high-temperature sterilization.

A few tips before preparing fermented foods:

▸ Sanitize all equipment by cleaning it thoroughly and then rinsing with a splash of distilled vinegar. Give the vinegar a good shake around all parts until it becomes frothy and then rinse with boiling water. Set aside to air dry.

▸ Avoid direct contact with metals (stainless steel is fine).

▸ Keep your hands clean, using fragrance-free bar soap—not hand sanitizer or anti-bacterial soap.

▸ The fermentation process should take place in a cool, well-ventilated space out of direct sunlight.

▸ Use organic, and preferably locally grown, produce. Rinse the produce with filtered water and set aside to air dry. Cabbage is the exception—simply remove the outer leaves and prepare it.

▸ Use kosher or unrefined (non-iodized) sea salt.

▸ If foam, scum, or mold appears on the surface during or after the fermentation process, skim it off and discard it. The food is safe underneath. Of course, if you're unsure then add it to your compost.

▸ If you open a container and it smells rotten, discard the contents and sanitize the jar.

Food Storage

FRESH PRODUCE

Place in a glass of water at room temperature and change the water every other day:

| Fresh herbs

At room temperature:

Avocado (when ripe or refrigerated when cut with the pit)	Apples
Eggplant	Bananas
Pumpkin	Citrus
Tomatoes	Kiwi
Winter squash	Pears
	Persimmons
	Pomegranates
	Stone fruits

In a cool (not refrigerated), dry place:

Garlic	Melons (until cut)
Onions, shallots	
Potatoes/Sweet potatoes	

Loose in the refrigerator crisper drawer:

Avocado (when cut and stored with pit)	Brussels sprouts (on the stalk)
Beets, carrots, radishes: Remove the leaves and store these in a cloth bag or dish towel; leave the roots loose in the drawer	Corn (unhusked); best eaten on day of purchase
	Cauliflower, cabbage
	Parsnips, rutabagas, turnips
	Zucchini

Refrigerated in a cloth bag or dish towel (make sure to wash produce bags every 2 weeks):

Asparagus	Green beans
Broccoli	Leafy greens
Brussels sprouts (loose)	Leeks
Celery	Green onions
Cucumbers	
Fennel	Grapes

Refrigerated in a brown paper bag:

Mushrooms	Berries
	Figs

Refrigerated in a glass or stainless steel container:

> **Cut fruits and vegetables** **Cherries**
> **Fermented foods (in glass only)**
> **Sprouts**

In the freezer in glass jars or stainless steel containers:

> **Any foods you want to enjoy out** **2 inches of air space to allow**
> **of season, such as berries, corn,** **for expansion so your jars don't**
> **fresh peas, etc.** **crack)**
> **Citrus peels (grate as needed)** **Lemongrass**
> **Chili peppers** **Turmeric**
> **Fresh ginger (grate as needed)** **Veggie scraps for Root-to-Leaf**
> **Soup Stock (page 215)**
> **Prepared smoothie packs** **Scraps for composting**
> **Homemade tomato sauce or**
> **soup stock (make sure to leave** **Ground flax seeds**

PANTRY ITEMS

Best stored at room temperature in airtight glass jars or stainless steel containers:

▸ Baking essentials: baking soda, baking powder, cocoa powder, dark chocolate, vanilla

▸ Dried fruits: apples, apricots, bananas, cranberries, coconut flakes, figs, goji berries, mango, pineapple, prunes, raisins

▸ Dried legumes: adzuki, black, black-eyed peas, borlotti, cannellini, chickpeas, lentils, lima, mung, navy, pinto, red kidney, split peas

▸ Flour: brown rice, buckwheat, chickpea (gram), cornmeal, spelt, whole wheat

▸ Nutritional yeast

▸ Nuts: almonds, Brazil nuts, cashews, macadamia nuts, peanuts, pecans, pistachios, walnuts

▸ Oils: avocado, coconut, olive, sesame

▸ Salt

▸ Black peppercorns

▸ Seeds: chia, whole flax seeds,* pepitas (pumpkin), sesame, sunflower

▸ Spices: caraway seeds, cardamom, cayenne pepper, cinnamon, coriander, cumin, garlic, mustard seeds, nutmeg, paprika, peppercorns, psyllium husk flakes or powder, red pepper flakes, turmeric, etc.

▸ Sweeteners: 100 percent pure maple syrup, coconut sugar, raw cane sugar

▸ Tahini and nut butters

- Tamari or gluten-free soy sauce
- Vinegar: apple cider, balsamic, rice, white
- Whole grains: bulgur wheat, oats, quinoa, rice, wheat berries

* Flax seed meal should be stored in the freezer to prevent it from becoming rancid.

LEFTOVERS

We always have leftovers (a.k.a. "bestovers"), and the quickest and easiest way we've been keeping them is to put a plate on top of the bowl. We even make use of small pots with lids placed directly into the refrigerator—making it that much easier to heat them up. Setting aside smaller portions in glass jars or stainless steel containers is great for grab-n-go meals.

BREAD | BAKED ITEMS | COOKIES | CRACKERS | SEAWEED | AND LOOSE-LEAF TEA

Generally best kept in airtight tins.

In the Kitchen

I've always loved watching food movies. There's a very memorable scene in the Japanese film *Tampopo* about kitchen efficiency and ensuring no movement or effort is wasted. I try to do this in my kitchen—perhaps by doing a little meal prep while cooking dinner, or by baking or roasting several things at the same time, while the oven is on. Many Asian kitchens don't have ovens, so steaming is a good alternative to roasting—and it's quicker too.

While cutting up vegetables, I set aside the scraps in a couple of bowls. One is filled with bits for soup stock and the other is filled with scraps for composting. After I finish cooking, they go into separate containers in my freezer. A zero-waste kitchen is really rewarding; it's also easy and efficient to use only one cutting board for many different dishes—and it saves on washing up, too (my least favorite part of cooking!). My friend's mother, Mama Wong, is so pro that she can cook six dishes for a single meal in the same pan!

The things I cook are generally easy to make. I use whatever I have on hand, and it's all seasoned simply. When using fresh ingredients, I prefer to let the natural flavors of the foods stand out, using minimal salt (more can always be added at the table to suit individual tastes). I also use minimal amounts of sugar, because too much salt and sugar gives me a massive headache. Headaches are no fun, and we all know that too much of either of those ingredients isn't good for your health.

Mindful Eating

▸ Drink a glass of water 15 minutes before a meal. It will help get your digestive juices flowing. You'll feel more full and eat less.

▸ Set aside a portion of your meal into single-serve containers and store them immediately. Use the leftovers for an easy packed lunch.

▸ Eat without distraction: with no computers, no TV, and no devices, and not on the move.

▸ Use all your senses—sight, smell, and touch—to enjoy your food. Even relaxing sounds can contribute to a mindful eating experience. Enjoy the taste and texture of each mouthful.

▸ Make single-serving snacks. You can easily portion out a large container of almonds or any other snack into individual snack-size containers. You'll be less tempted to take another baggie than you would be to reach in for another handful.

▸ Brush your teeth right after your last meal of the day to avoid late-night snack temptation.

▸ Chew your food (see the next section). Take your time, eat slowly, and put your fork down and pause for a breath or two between mouthfuls.

Chew Your Food

Digestion initially begins in the mouth. As you start to chew your food, digestive enzymes found in your saliva begin to break it down, preparing it for nutrient absorption. It's important to chew your food thoroughly to achieve maximum absorption of all its vitamins and minerals. To get into the habit of chewing food thoroughly, try counting the chews in each bite, aiming for 20 to 40 (yes, REALLY!) each time. Put your utensils down between bites to help you concentrate on chewing.

▸ Chew every mouthful at least 30 times, until the food becomes almost liquified.

▸ Chewing breaks down food, making it easier on the stomach and small intestine.

▸ Saliva assists in the digestion of carbohydrates and makes food more alkaline, which creates less gas.

▸ If you're under a lot of stress and pressure, remember when eating meals to take deep breaths, be mindful of your chewing, and let the simple act of chewing relax you. Taking the time to chew will help you enjoy the whole spectrum of tastes and aromas that make up your meal.

Preparing Foods in Advance

Making food from scratch doesn't mean being in the kitchen all day! You can plan to make ahead some elements for future meals while you're preparing tonight's meal, or make time on the weekend to prepare and portion out several meals. A spare 5 or 10 minutes can help you get a head start on any meal and help make putting meals together and healthy snacking easy, especially on busy days!

1. Clean and cut vegetables: Preparing your fruits and vegetables a few days in advance will help save time when it's time to cook and you'll always have a healthy snack or something to add to Sensational Salads (page 114) or Rainbowls (page 148) on hand.

2. Portion out your lunches and snacks: Divvy up the quinoa, greens, dressings, chopped vegetables, and snacks in containers so it's easy to "grab and go."

3. Make "smoothie packs" and freeze coconut milk: Chop up fruit and measure out baby greens into smoothie packs. Pop them into individual containers and store them in your freezer—they're very handy for easy morning starts!

4. Make salad dressings: Making larger portions of dressing in advance can save time.

5. Soak and prepare legumes, nuts, and grains.

Cooking Tools

Baking dish
Two baking sheets
Blender (glass)
Cast-iron skillet
Chopping board (bamboo)
Cooking utensils (wooden or stainless steel)
Fine-mesh sieve
Food processor (with a stainless steel bowl)
Glass or Mason jars, various sizes
Good knives, various sizes
Kitchen scissors
Mandolin
Measuring cup
Measuring spoons

Mixing bowls (glass or stainless steel), various sizes
Pots with lids, various sizes
Rice cooker
Steamer basket
Timer
Vegetable peeler
Wooden chopsticks or tongs
Parchment paper (unbleached; the brand If You Care is certified compostable)
Cheesecloth
Dish towels (organic cotton, hemp, or bamboo)
Reusable food-storage containers (glass or stainless steel)
Reusable shopping bags

Seasoning Cast Iron

A well-seasoned cast iron skillet is all you really need. Cooking in cast-iron boosts your iron intake and keeps foods hotter longer. Following are some tips on how to take care of this everlasting kitchen tool.

1. After purchasing, wash and dry your pan thoroughly with soapy water.

2. Rub a little olive oil all over the pan, including the handle. Rub and buff it until it doesn't look greasy.

3. Place the prepared pan in the oven at 450°F for 30 minutes (it might get smoky, so keep your kitchen well-ventilated). Remove from the oven and repeat steps 2 and 3 three more times.

5. To clean your cast-iron skillet after using it, wash it well with water; you can use salt to scrub away any bits that are stuck to the pan. Dry it very thoroughly and then rub a bit of olive oil on until it doesn't look oily. Place it on the burner over high heat and heat it for 2 to 3 minutes. Store in a dry place.

HOW TO USE THIS BOOK

Each recipe has an ingredient list for you to choose from each section. Using the measurements provided in the ingredient list, you can either use all of the single ingredients listed or a combination of ingredients within each category. Stick with your favorites, adapt with the seasons, or try something new. I've shared an example for each recipe, using my own preferred combinations. Mix and match to find your perfect vinyasa!

START

Opposite: Cherry Chia Jam, page 42

NO-BAKE BREAKFAST BARS

Weekday mornings are a lot easier when you're prepared. I love using fresh, in-season fruits to make Chia Jam (page 42), and the versatility of nut butter is the best. With these bars, you get the classic flavor combination of peanut butter and jelly without all the processing and refined sugar. Pairing this with whole grains makes for an easy breakfast or snack.

MAKES 1 (10-INCH SQUARE) TRAY42

CHOOSE YOUR FAVORITE COMBINATION

BASE (2 cups)	NUTS or SEEDS (1 cup)	FRUIT, mashed (1 cup)
Oats	Almonds	Applesauce
	Cashews	Bananas
SWEETENER (½ cup)	Hazelnuts	Berries
Brown rice syrup	Peanuts	Chia Jam (page 42)
Dates	Pecans	
Dried figs	Walnuts	OPTIONAL (½ cup)
Raisins	or (½ cup)	Cacao nibs
	Nut butter (page 40)	Chia seeds
OIL (¼ cup)		Dark chocolate, chopped
Coconut, melted		Shredded coconut
Vegan butter		

PEANUT BUTTER AND RASPBERRY JAM BREAKFAST BARS

½ cup pitted dates

½ cup peanut Nut Butter (page 40)

¼ cup coconut oil, melted

2 cups old-fashioned rolled oats

1 cup raspberry Chia Jam (see my recipe on page 42, substitute raspberries for the cherries)

METHOD

In a food processor fitted with the "S" blade, combine the dates, peanut butter, and coconut oil and blend together until a paste forms. Add the oats and chia jam and pulse a few times until combined.

Press this mixture firmly and evenly into a 10-inch square baking dish lined with wax or parchment paper and freeze for 2 hours.

Slice into bars and wrap or pack them into handy portions. Store in the refrigerator.

NUT BUTTER

There's something to be said for one-ingredient recipes! Depending on what kind of blender or food processor you have, this one could take time, but be patient. Adding optional oil or flavors can help your nut butter blend better—as well as add to its complexity. Experiment with making your nut butter out of a variety of nuts.

MAKES 1 CUP

CHOOSE YOUR FAVORITE COMBINATION

NUTS (2 cups)

Almonds

Brazil nuts

Cashews

Hazelnuts

Macadamia nuts

Peanuts

Pecans

Pistachios (shelled)

Walnuts

OTHER FLAVORS, optional
(½ teaspoon or pinch)

Cacao powder

Ground cinnamon

Pure maple syrup

OIL, optional
(1–2 tablespoons)

Coconut

Nut

METHOD

In a blender or food processor fitted with the "S" blade, blend or process the nuts for 8 to 10 minutes, until they have broken down. Scrape down the sides of the processor and continue blending (you may have to do this several times). You can add a little oil to help the process along, although that is not necessary with more powerful blenders and food processors.

Keep blending until the mixture warms from the processing, the natural oils of the nuts have released, and the mixture is creamy and smooth. Depending on the appliance you're using, this can take up to 20 minutes.

Stir in any additional flavors at the end, if using. Transfer to an airtight glass jar and store in the refrigerator for up to 3 weeks. Best served at room temperature.

CHIA JAM

I had to include this recipe, as my first attempt to make something from scratch was the strawberry jam I made when I was nine. Of course, I knew nothing about chia seeds back then, but they're the perfect addition: they absorb the juice and provide a jammy texture, while also adding protein.

CHOOSE YOUR FAVORITE COMBINATION

FRESH FRUIT (2 cups)

Blackberries	Mangoes
Blueberries	Peaches
Cherries	Persimmons
Figs	Raspberries
Kiwis	Strawberries

**TO BIND
(2 tablespoons)**

Chia seeds

Flax seed meal

**SWEETNESS
(1 tablespoon)**

Brown rice syrup

Pure maple syrup

Raw cane sugar

CHERRY CHIA JAM

MAKES ABOUT 1½ CUPS

2 heaping cups fresh cherries

2 tablespoons chia seeds

1 tablespoon pure maple syrup

METHOD

Remove the stems and pits from the cherries.

Combine the ingredients in a blender or food processor fitted with the "S" blade and puree until smooth.

Set aside for 15 minutes before serving or transfer to an airtight glass jar and store in the refrigerator.

CHIA PUDDING

Mighty chia seeds are packed with protein, complex carbohydrates (the good ones), and a plethora of nutrients. Easy to digest and high in antioxidants, they provide energy to both mind and body. Chia puddings are easy to prepare in advance. They're extremely versatile and are healthy, substantial "bresserts" (desserts for breakfast) that are also incredibly fun to eat!

METHOD

In a small bowl or jar, stir together the liquid of your choice and the chia seeds. Set aside to rest at room temperature for 20 minutes or overnight in the refrigerator, until the mixture becomes a gelatinous pudding.

Divide into two bowls or jars. Add the crunch, creaminess, and fruit in order on top of the pudding or in layers. Serve immediately or cover and store in the refrigerator.

The jars can also be prepared in advance for an easy grab-and-go breakfast or snack.

**LIQUID BASE
(1 cup)**

Coconut Milk
(page 82)

Coffee

Freshly squeezed
citrus juice

Nut Milk
(page 82)

Smoothie

**CHIA SEEDS
(3 tablespoons)**

Black chia seeds

White chia seeds

CRUNCH (½ cup)

Coconut flakes

Granola
(page 50)

Nuts

Seeds

**CREAMINESS
(½ cup)**

Cashew Cream
(page 160)

Cashewgurt
(page 46)

Nice Cream
(page 226)

**FRUITS or VEGETABLES (1 cup/piece,
fresh or cooked)**

Apple

Bananas

Beets

Berries

Cherries

Figs

Grapefruit

Grapes

Kiwis

Mangoes

Melons

Oranges

Peaches

Persimmons

Pineapple

Pitayas

Pomegranates

Sweet potatoes

KIWI CHIA PUDDING

MAKES 2 SERVINGS

Freshly squeezed juice of
2 oranges (about 1 cup)

2 kiwis (1 for blending and
1 for topping)

1 kale leaf, stem removed

3 tablespoons chia seeds

Cashewgurt (page 46), Granola
(page 50), and fresh fruit for
topping

METHOD

In a blender, combine the orange juice, 1 of the kiwis, and the kale leaf and puree until smooth. Stir in the chia seeds and set aside to rest at room temperature for 20 minutes or refrigerate overnight, until the mixture becomes a gelatinous pudding.

Divide into two bowls or jars. Add the cashewgurt, granola, and fresh fruit on top of the pudding or in layers. Serve immediately or cover and store in the refrigerator.

Here are some chia pudding creations by:

ROW 1: @thejamlab @naturallyzuzu @wifemamafoodie
ROW 2: @plantbasedartist @frei_style @choosingchia
ROW 3: @monsflavors @rachels.fit.kitchen @juutlovesfood

More inspiration can be found on Instagram #chiapudfun

CASHEWGURT

Maybe it's just me, but it seems really difficult to find good vegan yogurt. I've taken to making my own, and I find that cashews, truly the best substitute for dairy, work very well. This recipe is also great because there's no need for gums or thickeners, and you prepare it right on your countertop. Homemade yogurt just tastes better, and it also saves tremendously on plastic waste. If you do purchase yogurt, buy large containers rather than individual portions, and always recycle or upcycle your containers.

MAKES ¾ CUP

1 cup raw cashews

⅔ cup filtered water

1 tablespoon pure maple syrup

1 probiotic capsule

2 teaspoons freshly squeezed
  lemon juice or to taste

METHOD

Cover the cashews with the filtered water and set aside to soak overnight.

In a blender, combine the cashews, their soaking water, and the syrup and puree until smooth. Transfer to a glass jar. Open the probiotic capsule and stir its powder into the cashew mixture until well combined.

Place the jar's lid slightly askew, leaving space for air to circulate, or cover with cheesecloth. Place in an out-of-the-way spot on your kitchen counter where it can sit undisturbed for 24 hours.

Stir in the lemon juice to taste. If the mixture has thickened and tastes sufficiently sour, transfer the Cashewgurt to an airtight container and store in the refrigerator. Otherwise, let this ferment for one more day. Use within 3 days.

FRENCH TOAST

Even though I started using flax- and chia-seed "eggs" in my baking, I never thought about using them for a French toast batter. This really works as well as the original. Be generous with your fresh ingredient toppings to boost the nutrients.

CHOOSE YOUR FAVORITE COMBINATION

BREAD (4–6 slices)

Brioche

Challah

Sourdough pullman

**OIL FOR FRYING
(1–2 tablespoons)**

Coconut

Vegan butter

LIQUID (1 cup)

Plant Milk (page 82)

+

1 tablespoon flax seed meal

+

¼ teaspoon ground turmeric

+

1 tablespoon pure maple syrup

FLAVOR (2 teaspoons)

SWEET

Citrus zest

Ground cardamom

Ground cinnamon

Freshly grated ginger

Freshly grated nutmeg

Vanilla

SAVORY

Garlic powder

Green onions

Tamari or soy sauce

**FRUITS or VEGETABLES
(½ cup, fresh or cooked)**

Apples

Bananas

Beets

Berries

Cherries

Figs

Grapefruit

Kiwis

Mangoes

Oranges

Peaches

Persimmons

Pineapple

Pitayas

Pomegranate arils

Sweet potatoes (cooked)

TOPPINGS (¼ cup)

Cashewgurt (page 46)

Coconut flakes

Granola (page 50)

Nuts

Seeds

DRIZZLE

Brown rice syrup

Cashew Cream (page 160)

Nut butter

Pure maple syrup

Raw chocolate

Salted Caramel Sauce (page 49)

Tahini

Toffee Sauce (page 243)

SWEET POTATO AND SALTED CARAMEL FRENCH TOAST

MAKES 2 TO 3 SERVINGS

1 cup Coconut Milk (page 82)

1 tablespoon flax seed meal

1 tablespoon pure maple syrup

1 teaspoon vanilla extract

1 teaspoon freshly grated orange zest

½ teaspoon ground cinnamon

¼ teaspoon ground turmeric

4–6 slices bread

2 tablespoons coconut oil

½ cup diced and steamed sweet potato for topping

¼ cup Salted Caramel Sauce (recipe follows) for topping

¼ cup pecan halves for topping

Chia seeds for topping

METHOD

In a large, shallow-rimmed dish, mix the coconut milk, flax seed meal, maple syrup, vanilla extract, orange zest, cinnamon, and turmeric. Set aside for 5 to 7 minutes.

Soak each slice of the bread in the mixture, allowing each side to absorb and be coated with the batter.

In a large skillet over medium heat, warm 1 tablespoon of the coconut oil until the surface is evenly coated. Place slices of the soaked bread in the pan and cook for 2 to 3 minutes on each side, until golden. Remove from the skillet and transfer to a platter.

Repeat with the remaining slices, adding the remaining coconut oil to the pan as needed. Remove from the heat. Pile on the sweet potato, salted caramel sauce, pecan halves, and chia seeds and enjoy!

SALTED CARAMEL SAUCE

1 cup pitted dates

½ cup raw cashews

2 cups boiling water

2 tablespoons warm pure maple syrup, plus more as desired

2 tablespoons coconut oil, melted

2 tablespoons warm water or more, if needed, to achieve desired consistency

½ teaspoon salt or to taste

METHOD

Place the dates and cashews in a medium bowl and pour the boiling water over them. Set aside to soak, completely covered, for 15 minutes. Drain and transfer to a blender. Add the maple syrup and coconut oil and blend until smooth. Add the warm water or more syrup, if desired, to reach a pourable consistency. Season with the salt. Use immediately or store refrigerated in an airtight glass jar.

GOOD-FOR-YOU GRANOLA

Granola is easy to make, so it's no wonder there are so many different varieties available on supermarket shelves. Making it yourself is a fun way to get creative with flavors, and it's so much more cost effective than purchasing it in tiny packs.

CHOOSE YOUR FAVORITE COMBINATION

BASE (3 cups)

Large unsweetened coconut flakes

Rolled oats

RAW NUTS + SEEDS (1 cup chopped)

Almonds

Macadamia nuts

Pecans

Pepitas (pumpkin)

Pistachios (shelled)

Sesame

Sunflower

Walnuts

OIL (3 tablespoons)

Coconut, melted

Olive

Sunflower seed

SWEETNESS (3 tablespoons)

Brown rice syrup

Pure maple syrup

Raw cane sugar

LIQUID (3 tablespoons)

Beet juice

Filtered water

Freshly squeezed orange juice

FLAVOR (1–2 teaspoons)

Freshly grated ginger

Freshly grated nutmeg

Ground allspice

Ground cinnamon

Orange zest

Vanilla extract

ADDITIONS (¼ cup)

Chia seeds

Dark chocolate, chopped

Dried fruit

Hemp seeds

Shredded coconut

SUNSHINE GRANOLA

MAKES 7 TO 12 SERVINGS (AROUND 4 CUPS)

3 cups large unsweetened coconut flakes

½ cup walnuts

½ cup sunflower seeds

1 teaspoon freshly grated nutmeg

1 (1-inch) piece ginger, freshly grated

3 tablespoons coconut oil, melted

3 tablespoons pure maple syrup

3 tablespoons freshly squeezed orange juice

Freshly grated zest of 1 orange

¼ cup golden raisins

METHOD

In a food processor fitted with the "S" blade, pulse together the coconut flakes, nuts, and seeds until the pieces break down (if you don't have a food processor, roughly chop them with a large knife).

NOTE: You can stop here, add the raisins, and have a lovely muesli/raw granola (rawnola), but lightly toasting granola with a little sweetener really brings out the flavors of the ingredients.

Preheat the oven to 275°F. Evenly spread the mixture on a baking sheet lined with parchment paper. Drizzle the coconut oil, syrup, freshly squeezed orange juice, and orange zest over the mixture, tossing this together until it is thoroughly coated.

Bake for 30 to 35 minutes, or until the mixture is dry. Toss the mixture around twice while it bakes to ensure it dries thoroughly. Remove from the oven and set aside to cool completely.

Add the raisins and store at room temperature in an airtight jar.

WHOLE-GRAIN PORRIDGE

On the weekends, I often prepare a batch of whole grains with water only, rather than with soup stock or seasoned with salt. This way I can heat it up quickly in the morning with some Plant Milk (page 82) and enjoy a hearty porridge with some fresh fruit and nuts.

CHOOSE YOUR FAVORITE COMBINATION

GRAINS
(1 cup, cooked)

Amaranth

Buckwheat

Millet

Quinoa

Rice

Rolled oats

Steel-cut oats

ADDED PROTEIN
(3 tablespoons)

Plant Milk Pulp
(page 83)

LIQUID (1 cup)

Plant Milk
(page 82)

SPICE
(¼–½ teaspoon)

Freshly grated
nutmeg

Freshly grated
ginger

Ground cardamom

Ground cinnamon

Ground turmeric

Pumpkin pie

TOPPINGS (1 cup)

Apples

Bananas

Berries

Carrots

Corn

Figs

Oranges

Pears

Persimmons

Plums

Pumpkin

Sweet potatoes

Zucchini

SPRINKLES

Chia seeds

Chili pepper flakes

Coconut flakes

Coconut sugar

Dried fruit

Granola (page 50)

Green onions

Nuts, chopped

Orange zest

Pomegranate arils

Seeds

Spices

DRIZZLE

Brown rice syrup

Cashew Cream
(page 160)

Nut butter (page
40)

Pure maple syrup

Raw chocolate

Tahini

TAHINI MILLET PORRIDGE

MAKES 1 SERVING

1 cup cooked millet

1½ cups Coconut Milk (page 82)

½ teaspoon ground cinnamon

1 blood orange, sliced

2 tablespoons pecan halves

1 tablespoon cacao nibs

1 teaspoon black sesame seeds

Tahini for topping

METHOD

In a small saucepan over low heat, warm the millet, coconut milk, and cinnamon. Remove from the heat and transfer to a bowl.

Top with the orange slices, pecans, cacao nibs, sesame seeds, and tahini and eat while hot for a cozy start to the day.

PANCAKES

As a child, every Sunday my dad would make us Bisquick pancakes in the shapes of Mickey Mouse—the letter "C" for me and "M" for my sister. Later in life, I learned that making pancakes from scratch was just as easy—without any funky additives. I've adapted this recipe many times over the years and now have a favorite: this whole-grain, vegan version. Chocolate with cherries is one of my favorite flavor combinations, or mix and match from the list below for a delicious start (or end) to the day.

CHOOSE YOUR FAVORITE COMBINATION

FLOUR (1 cup)

Buckwheat

Chickpea (gram)

Oat

Spelt

Whole wheat

+

(1 tablespoon)

Baking powder

OPTIONAL

1 teaspoon spice of choice

2 tablespoons cocoa powder

LIQUID (1 cup)

Plant Milk (page 82)

OIL (1 tablespoon plus more for frying)

Coconut

Sunflower seed

Vegan butter

TO BIND

1 tablespoon chia seeds + 3 tablespoons filtered water

1 tablespoon flax seed meal + 3 tablespoons filtered water

¼ cup freshly grated apple

¼ cup mashed ripe banana

¼ cup sweet potato or pumpkin puree

3 tablespoons Aquafaba (page 27), well-beaten (for fluffy pancakes)

TOPPINGS (1 cup/piece)

Apples

Bananas

Beets

Berries

Cherries

Figs

Kiwis

Lemons

Mangoes

Oranges

Peaches

Persimmons

Pineapple

Pitayas

Pomegranate arils

Sweet potatoes

DRIZZLE

Brown rice syrup

Cashew Cream (page 160)

Nut butter (page 40)

Pure maple syrup

Raw chocolate

Salted Caramel Sauce (page 49)

Tahini

Toffee Sauce (page 243)

CHOCOLATE CHERRY PANCAKES

MAKES 8 TO 9 (3½-INCH) PANCAKES

⅔ cup spelt flour
⅓ cup buckwheat flour
1 tablespoon baking powder
1 cup Cashew Milk (page 82)
¼ cup freshly grated apple

3 tablespoons melted coconut oil, divided
1 cup sliced cherries for topping
Raw chocolate for drizzling

METHOD

Combine the flours and the baking powder in a large bowl. Add the cashew milk, apple, and 1 tablespoon of melted coconut oil and stir until just combined. The batter should be pourable, but it can be lumpy.

In a large skillet over medium-high heat, melt another tablespoon of the coconut oil until the skillet is well coated. Pour three (¼-cup) portions of the batter into the oiled skillet, with 1 inch of space between each pancake.

In a small bowl or saucepan, melt the raw chocolate for drizzling.

After 2 to 3 minutes, when the pancakes are golden brown on the bottom, flip them over and cook for 1 more minute. Remove from the skillet, set aside on a plate, and cover with a clean dish towel to keep warm.

Add the remaining coconut oil to the pan and repeat until all the pancake batter has been used. Remove from the heat.

Top the pancakes with the sliced cherries and drizzle with the raw chocolate.

NOTE: Pancakes don't have to be sweet. For a savory version, green onion pancakes are a favorite!

MUFFINS

Any way to get fresh vegetables on the breakfast table is a win in my book! Once, I purchased a blueberry muffin with only one blueberry; the disappointment was real. I love to add lots of fresh ingredients to my homemade muffins. In particular, I love cardamom for its taste of coziness on dark winter mornings. Although it's not necessary, it's nice to have some extra nuts and seeds handy to sprinkle on top.

CHOOSE YOUR FAVORITE COMBINATION

FLAVOR (2 cups)

Apples, diced

Blueberries

Cranberries

(or 1 cup grated)

Carrots

Summer squash

Zucchini

FLOUR (2 cups)

Buckwheat

Chickpea (gram)

Oats

Spelt

Whole wheat

+

(2 teaspoons)

Baking powder

TO BIND

1 tablespoon chia seeds + 3 tablespoons filtered water

1 tablespoon flax seed meal + 3 tablespoons filtered water

¼ cup grated apple

¼ cup ripe banana, mashed

¼ cup sweet potato or pumpkin puree

3 tablespoons Aquafaba (page 27)

SWEET (¼–½ cup)

Brown rice syrup

Pure maple syrup

Raw cane sugar

OIL (¼ cup)

Coconut

Sunflower seed

Vegan butter

+

(¼ cup)

Nut Milk (page 82)

EXTRAS (1–2 teaspoons)

Freshly grated mace

Freshly grated nutmeg

Ground allspice

Ground cardamom

Ground cinnamon

Ground ginger

Pumpkin pie spice

CRANBERRY SQUASH MUFFINS

MAKES 6 TO 8

FOR THE MUFFINS

½ cup freshly grated summer squash

¼ cup butternut squash puree

¼ cup coconut butter, softened

¼ cup pure maple syrup

¼ cup raw cane sugar

1½ cups gluten-free oats

½ cup buckwheat flour

2 teaspoons baking powder

1 teaspoon ground cardamom

¼ cup Almond Milk (page 82)

1½ cups fresh cranberries

FOR THE TOPPING

½ cup chopped walnuts

2 tablespoons chia seeds

METHOD

Make the muffins: Preheat the oven to 400°F. Line a muffin pan with muffin cups or parchment paper squares.

In a large bowl, beat together the summer and butternut squash, coconut butter, maple syrup, and sugar. Add the oats, flour, baking powder, and cardamom to this mixture and beat until well combined. Stir in the almond milk and then the cranberries. Scoop even portions of the batter into the prepared muffin pan.

Make the topping: In a small bowl, mix together the walnuts and chia seeds. Sprinkle the topping on the muffins, pressing them into the batter slightly.

Bake for 15 to 20 minutes. Remove from the oven and set aside to cool completely.

Serve or store in an airtight container.

AVOCADO BOATS

Save time on washing up in the morning. These avocado "eggs" can easily be filled with the smallest bits of leftovers, as well as with the easy Mock "Tuna" Salad recipe that follows.

AVOCADO BOATS

MAKES 1 SERVING

1 ripe avocado
Mock "Tuna" Salad (recipe
    follows)

Fennel microgreens
Freshly ground black pepper

METHOD

Halve the avocado and remove and discard the pit. Fill with the Mock "Tuna" Salad and microgreens and season with the black pepper.

BASE

1 avocado

FILLING

Carrot Lox (page 65)

Hummus (page 98)

Leafy greens, shredded

Leftover Chili (page 201)

Mushroom Tapenade
(page 109)

Nut Cheese (page 101)

Pulses (cooked; page 26)

Quinoa (cooked)

Roasted Eggplant Dip
(page 170)

Salsa (page 176)

Tofu Scramble (page 66)

Tomatuna (page 142)

SPRINKLES

Dukkah

Fresh chives

Fresh herbs

Freshly ground black
pepper

Freshly squeezed citrus
juice and zest

Hemp seeds

Microgreens

Pesto (page 164)

Salt

Sesame seeds

Spices

Sprouts (page 24)

**OPTIONAL
CONDIMENTS**

Cashew Cream (page 160)

Garlic Mayonnaise
(page 62)

Hoisin Sauce (page 145)

Homemade Harissa
(page 126)

Nut Butter (page 40)

Pesto (page 164)

Raw Marinara Sauce
(page 139)

MOCK "TUNA" SALAD

MAKES 2 TO 4 SERVINGS

1 cup cooked chickpeas
(page 26)

2 tablespoons Oil-Free Mayonnaise (recipe follows)

2 dill pickle slices, chopped

1 teaspoon pickle juice

¼ teaspoon salt

2 tablespoons fresh chives, finely
chopped

Red pepper flakes for sprinkling
(optional)

METHOD

In a food processor fitted with the "S" blade, combine the chickpeas, oil-free mayonnaise, pickles, pickle juice, and salt and pulse a few times until just combined (the
mixture should be broken up, but should have a few large pieces).

Transfer to a bowl. Stir in the chives and sprinkle with the red pepper flakes.

Serve immediately or store refrigerated in an airtight container for up to 5 days.

OIL-FREE MAYONNAISE

MAKES ABOUT ¾ CUP

1 cup cashews, soaked for 3
    hours or overnight, rinsed and
    drained
¼ cup cauliflower florets
¼ cup filtered water
1 tablespoon apple cider vinegar

1 teaspoon Dijon mustard
½ teaspoon pure maple syrup
Freshly squeezed juice of
    ½–1 lemon or to taste
Salt to taste

METHOD

In a blender, combine the cashews, cauliflower, water, vinegar, mustard, and maple syrup. Add the juice of ½ the lemon and blend until smooth. Taste and season with the salt; add more of the lemon juice as desired.

Use immediately or store refrigerated in a clean airtight glass jar for up to 10 days.

VARIATIONS:

Avocado Cream: Combine ½ cup oil-free mayonnaise with 1 mashed avocado

Garlic Mayonnaise: Combine ½ cup oil-free mayonnaise with 1 clove finely chopped garlic

Spicy Mayonnaise: Combine ½ cup oil-free mayonnaise with 2 to 3 teaspoons Homemade Harissa (page 126) or to taste

BAGEL BREAKFAST

Because we live in New York City, bagels, lox, and cream cheese have been at the core of our special holiday or birthday breakfasts for years now. Traditionally, Chinese vegan food is unrecognizably brown and smothered in sauces that are full of MSG. I never understood why anyone would want mock "duck" or other imitation meats until I made my Carrot Lox (recipe follows). I didn't think I'd be able to call it lox, but it really does have the same taste and texture as smoked salmon. Dulse flakes are a red, edible seaweed that's ground up; they are typically used as a natural salt alternative. In this recipe, they give the carrots a flavor of the sea—along with B vitamins, iodine, and iron.

CHOOSE YOUR FAVORITE COMBINATION

BASE	CREAMINESS	TOPPINGS	
Bagels	Cashew Cream (page 160)	Arugula	Jalapeño peppers
Essential Loaf (page 73)	Cashewgurt (page 46)	Avocados	Lettuce
Flatbreads (page 168)	Nut Cheese (page 101)	Capers	Radishes
Seeded Crackers (page 102)		Carrot Lox (recipe follows)	Red onions
Sourdough rolls		Cucumbers	Spinach
Sweet Potato Toasts (page 109)		Fresh dill	Tomatoes

CARROT "LOX" BAGEL BREAKFAST

MAKES 4 SERVINGS

FOR THE LOX

2 large carrots

4 tablespoons olive oil

1 teaspoon rice vinegar

1 teaspoon dulse flakes

½ teaspoon salt

¼ teaspoon smoked paprika

3 tablespoons fresh dill

¼ teaspoon freshly ground black pepper

Freshly squeezed lemon juice to taste

Salt to taste

FOR SERVING

2–4 bagels

Cashew Cheese (page 101)

Red onion, fresh dill, and freshly ground black pepper for garnish

METHOD

Make the lox: Peel the carrots and then cut them into ribbons using the same peeler.

Set up a steamer: Place a large pot with a steamer insert over high heat. Add 1 inch of water to the pot and bring the water to a boil. Add the carrot ribbons and cover and steam for 5 minutes, or until slightly softened. Remove from the heat.

In a large bowl, combine 2 tablespoons of the olive oil, rice vinegar, dulse flakes, salt, and paprika. Add the steamed carrot ribbons and toss until well coated. Set aside to marinate for 30 minutes or overnight.

Preheat the oven to 375°F. On a large piece of parchment paper placed on a baking sheet, arrange the marinated carrots on one half of the sheet, with the strips slightly overlapping one another. Fold the unfilled portion of the parchment paper over, covering the carrot layer. Fold the three open edges over to close the parcel. Bake for 15 to 17 minutes. Remove from the oven and set aside to cool before unwrapping.

Toss with the remaining 2 tablespoons of olive oil, the dill, and the black pepper. Season lightly with the lemon juice and salt.

To serve: Serve with the bagels and cashew cheese and garnish with the red onion, fresh dill, and black pepper. Store any remaining Carrot Lox in the refrigerator in an airtight jar or container.

TOFU SCRAMBLE

In Hong Kong and China, homemade tofu is readily available—package free—in the wet markets. Happily, I found a popular tofu stand in NYC's Chinatown and now bring my own container for them to fill up. When compiling the recipes for the first issue of my #plasticfreefoodie eMagazine, I was surprised to learn from foodies based in Germany that packaging-free homemade tofu is readily available there, too! This recipe is a bit of an East-meets-West meal, as it contains one of my favorite Chinese foods on a piece of toast. I love this as a protein-packed brunch or post-workout snack. I found the Sichuan peppercorns at a bulk spice shop at Chelsea Market, but any other peppercorns will work, too.

CHOOSE YOUR FAVORITE COMBINATION

TOFU (4 ounces)

+

1 tablespoon nutritional yeast

+

¼ teaspoon salt

+

¼ teaspoon ground turmeric

SEASONING (2 teaspoons)

Curry powder

Garlic powder

Ground coriander

Ground cumin

Onion powder

Paprika

Peppercorns, crushed

Smoked paprika

VEGETABLES (¼ cup)

Bell peppers

Chard

Fresh chives

Green onion

Kale

Mushrooms

Spinach

Watercress

BASE

Bagel

Essential Loaf (page 73)

Flatbreads (page 168)

Flour Tortillas (page 174)

Seeded Crackers (page 102)

Sourdough bread

Sweet Potato Toasts (page 109)

MA PO TOFU SCRAMBLE

MAKES 1 SERVING

1 tablespoon olive oil

4 ounces firm tofu, crumbled

1 green onion, finely chopped

1 (¼-inch) piece ginger, freshly grated

1 teaspoon Sichuan peppercorns, crushed

½ teaspoon Aleppo pepper

¼ teaspoon garlic powder

¼ teaspoon salt

1 kale leaf, stem removed and shredded

1 piece sourdough bread, toasted

METHOD

In a small skillet over medium-high heat, warm the olive oil. Add the crumbled tofu and cook for 3 to 5 minutes, stirring frequently. Add the green onion, ginger, crushed Sichuan peppercorns, Aleppo pepper, garlic powder, and salt and cook for 1 more minute. Remove from the heat and toss in the shredded kale.

Place the toast on a plate and pile the contents of the skillet on top of it. Serve immediately.

FRITTATA

This dish is based on *socca*, a chickpea flatbread found in Italy and France. The addition of the cauliflower adds to the depth of the dish's flavors—and boosts nutrients as well. This is a versatile vehicle for repurposing leftovers and highlighting in-season vegetables. It makes a handy protein for a packed lunch.

CHOOSE YOUR FAVORITE COMBINATION

BASE	SEASONING	FILLING 1 (1½ cups)	CONDIMENTS (to taste)
1 cup chickpea (gram) flour	1 tablespoon nutritional yeast	Bell peppers	Cashew Cream (page 160)
+	+	Fennel	Chutney (page 131)
1¼ cups boiling water	1 teaspoon turmeric powder	Onion	Homemade Harissa (page 126)
+	+	Potato	Hoisin Sauce (page 145)
1 cup cauliflower, riced	½ teaspoon garlic powder	FILLING 2 (1½ cups)	Kimchi (page 153)
+	+	Broccoli	Oil-Free Mayonnaise (page 62)
2 tablespoons olive oil	¼ teaspoon freshly ground black pepper	Corn	Pesto (page 164)
	+	Fresh herbs	Pickles (page 151)
	1 teaspoon salt	Leafy greens	Salsa (page 176)
		Mushrooms	
		Zucchini	

FRESH HERB AND FENNEL FRITTATA

MAKES 2 SERVINGS

FOR THE BASE

1 cup chickpea (gram) flour

1¼ cups boiling water

1 cup cauliflower, riced

2 tablespoons olive oil

1 tablespoon nutritional yeast

1 teaspoon turmeric powder

½ teaspoon garlic powder

¼ teaspoon freshly ground black
  pepper

1 teaspoon salt

FOR THE FILLING

1 tablespoon olive oil

1 fennel bulb, thinly diced

1 shallot, thinly sliced

2 cups finely chopped fresh herbs
  (I like to use a mix of parsley,
  basil, and cilantro)

METHOD

Make the base: Blend or process together all of the base ingredients until smooth. Set aside to rest at room temperature for 30 minutes or covered and refrigerated for up to 12 hours.

Preheat the oven to 450°F.

Make the filling: In a cast-iron skillet over high heat, warm the olive oil. Add the fennel and shallot and sauté for 5 to 7 minutes, or until softened and browned. Add the chopped herbs and sauté for 2 more minutes. Remove from the heat.

Pour the chickpea batter into the skillet and bake for 7 to 10 minutes, or until set. Remove the skillet from the oven and eat this directly from the pan, or slice and serve.

BREAKFAST FRITTERS

Having vegetables in the morning makes it super easy to get your five-a-day. You can also prepare a big batch of these and stash them in the freezer; they heat up quickly on busy mornings. This is a version with turnips, a spin-off on Chinese *lo bak go* (daikon "cake"), which is one of our dim sum favorites. Turnips can be bitter though, so I combined it with a white-fleshed Japanese sweet potato that balances the flavors. You can also serve this with Hoisin Sauce (page 145).

CHOOSE YOUR FAVORITE COMBINATION

BASE (1 pound)	VEGETABLE (4 ounces, julienned or grated)	AROMATICS (1–2 tablespoons)
Apples	Apples	Fresh chives
Beets	Asparagus	Freshly grated ginger
Butternut squash	Carrots	Garlic
Carrots	Leeks	Green onion
Celery root	Parsnips	Leeks
Daikon radishes	Snow peas	Onion
Parsnips	Zucchini	Shallots
Potatoes		
Sweet potatoes	**SEASONING**	**TO BIND (¼ cup)**
Turnips	2 tablespoons nutritional yeast	Brown rice flour
		Flaxseed meal
OIL (2–4 tablespoons)	+	Spelt flour
Coconut	2–3 teaspoons spice, mixed	Whole wheat flour
Light sesame		
Olive	+	
	½ teaspoon salt	

TURNIP AND SWEET POTATO BREAKFAST FRITTERS

MAKES 6 TO 8

1 turnip, peeled and grated

1 Japanese sweet potato, peeled and grated

½ cup snow peas, thinly sliced

1 green onion, chopped

¼ cup brown rice flour

2 tablespoons light sesame oil

2 tablespoons nutritional yeast

1 teaspoon garlic powder

1 teaspoon ground coriander

½ teaspoon salt

METHOD

Preheat the oven to 400°F and line a baking sheet with parchment paper.

In a large bowl, combine the grated turnip, sweet potato, snow peas, and green onion. Add the brown rice flour, sesame oil, nutritional yeast, garlic powder, coriander, and salt and toss well. Set aside to rest for 30 minutes.

Scoop the mixture into ¼-cup patties and flatten them on the prepared baking sheet. Continue until all of the batter has been used. Bake for 20 to 30 minutes, flipping them over once. Remove from the oven.

Serve immediately.

ESSENTIAL LOAF

This incredibly easy-to-make, hearty, tasty, and nutritious loaf is derived from the recipe for the "Life-Changing Loaf" by Sarah Britton at My New Roots. Here, there's no need for the yeast and chemistry of traditional breadmaking. Simply mix the ingredients together, let the mixture rest, and then bake! It's a perfect gluten-free option, and great if you're just tired of plain old sliced bread. I chose this flavor combination because it reminds me of the onion-herb bread my mother used to make.

CHOOSE YOUR FAVORITE COMBINATION

BASE

2 cups gluten-free oats

+

3 tablespoons chia seeds

+

¼ cup flax seeds

+

¼ cup psyllium husk

+

1 teaspoon salt

SEEDS + NUTS (2 cups)

Almonds

Macadamia nuts

Pecans

Pepitas (pumpkin seeds)

Pistachios (shelled)

Sesame

Sunflower

Walnuts

OIL (3 tablespoons)

Coconut

Olive

Sesame, light

Sunflower seed

**OPTIONAL SPICES
(1 tablespoon)**

Cloves

Five-spice powder

Fresh cilantro

Freshly grated ginger

Freshly ground black pepper

Garlic powder

Ground allspice

Ground cardamom

Ground cinnamon

**OPTIONAL ADDITIONS
(¼ cup)**

Fresh rosemary

Fresh sage

Fresh thyme

Green onions

Jalapeño peppers

Nutritional yeast

Olives

Onions

Pesto (page 164)

LIQUID (2 cups)

Chai tea

Earl Grey tea

Filtered water

Root-to-Leaf Stock (page 215)

GREEN ONION AND SESAME LOAF

MAKES 1 LOAF

2 cups gluten-free oats

2 cups warm filtered water

1½ cups almonds

½ cup chopped green onions
   (5 stalks)

¼ cup flax seeds

¼ cup psyllium husk

¼ cup sunflower seeds

¼ cup white sesame seeds

3 tablespoons chia seeds

3 tablespoons light sesame oil

1 tablespoon chopped fresh
   cilantro

1 teaspoon salt

METHOD

Grease or line a loaf pan with parchment paper.

In a large bowl, combine all of the ingredients and set aside for 10 minutes, until the liquid is all absorbed.

Pour the mixture into the prepared loaf pan, spreading it out evenly and making a smooth, even surface on top. Set aside at room temperature for at least 1 hour or overnight, if possible.

Preheat the oven to 375°F.

Bake for 40 to 50 minutes. Remove from the oven and set aside to cool for 15 minutes.

Turn out the loaf onto a cooling rack and set aside to cool completely before slicing. Be patient! Slice and serve; if storing, freeze for optimal freshness.

SIPS

TEAS AND HERBAL INFUSIONS

Did you know that many tea leaves are packed without being cleaned? That means there are pesticides and chemicals steeping in your cup or pot of tea. Plus, some tea bags are made with plastic, and when these come in contact with heat, they're likely to leach out for you to ingest. I like to stick to natural infusions, thanks!

One of my favorite food memories is enjoying fresh, garden-grown lemon verbena tea after dinner in the summertime. These plants can easily grow indoors or outdoors. If you can't grow your own, buy your herbs in season at the farmers' market. Wash and dry the stems thoroughly and store them in the freezer for use anytime.

CHOOSE YOUR FAVORITE COMBINATION

WATER (1 cup)	Lemongrass	FRESH FRUITS AND ROOTS (3–5 slices)	SEEDS AND SPICES (1–4 pieces)
Boiling water	Lemon verbena		
	Marjoram	Apple peels	Caraway seeds
FRESH HERBS AND FLOWERS (¼–½ cup chopped)	Oregano	Freshly grated ginger	Cardamom pods
	Parsley		Cayenne pepper
	Peppermint	Ground turmeric	Cinnamon stick
Basil	Perilla	Lemon peel	Cloves
Chamomile	Rose petals	Orange peel	Fennel seeds
Cilantro	Rosehips		Freshly ground black pepper
Fennel	Rosemary	OPTIONAL SWEETENER (to taste)	Star anise
Lavender	Sage		
Lemon balm	Thyme		

METHOD

HOT TEA: Simply place a stem or two (about ¼ cup) of an herb or flower into a cup or coffee press, pour in some boiling water, and set aside to steep for 3 to 5 minutes. You can refill with more hot water a few times before discarding the herb or flower.

SUN TEA: Place the ingredients in a glass jar. Fill with filtered room-temperature water and set aside to sit in the sunshine all day. This is the best way to infuse a floral tea.

NOTE: Crushing herbs will help bring out their flavor.

FRUITY WATER

Did you know that 60 to 75 percent of your body is made up of water? So if you're not feeling right—backache, headache, digestive issues, or are always tired—perhaps you're not getting enough H_2O. On average, women should be drinking 74 fluid ounces (9 cups) a day, while men should aim for 101 fluid ounces (12½ cups) a day. Drink a glass of water when you feel like snacking and wait a few minutes to see if you're still hungry. Also, drinking water anywhere from 15 minutes to 1 hour before a meal aids digestion. Instead of reaching for a soda or a store-bought, sweetened, artificially colored, and artificially flavored drink, liven up your water with natural flavors. Not only do you get delicious flavor, you also benefit from the intake of added nutrients.

CHOOSE YOUR FAVORITE COMBINATION

LIQUID BASE (4 cups)		FRESH GREENS (½ cup chopped)	OTHER
Filtered water	Grapefruit	Basil	Cayenne pepper
Fresh coconut water	Kiwis	Cilantro	Freshly grated ginger
Sparkling water	Lemons	Lemon verbena	Ground cinnamon
	Limes	Mint	Ice, optional
FRUIT (1 cup)	Oranges	Rosemary	Jalapeño peppers
Blackberries	Pineapple	Sage	Rose petals
Cucumbers	Raspberries	Thyme	
	Strawberries		
	Watermelon		

METHOD
Simply fill a large glass pitcher or water bottle with water and a handful of fruit or fresh herbs and set aside to infuse. Refill throughout the day.

PLANT MILK

Homemade cashew milk is one of the first recipes I teach to clients in my meal prep and reboot programs. With only three ingredients, it's such an easy way to make sure you can always have milk on hand. Cashews are particularly great because there's no need to strain them. For all other nuts, strain the liquid from the pulp for a smooth, and not gritty, milk. You can use this pulp for porridge or smoothies; as a flour for battering Veggie Fries (page 137); or in baking treats. The walnut-sesame combination reminds me of a healthier version of a classic Chinese dessert.

CHOOSE YOUR FAVORITE COMBINATION

BASE (1 cup)

Almonds

Brazil nuts

Cashews

Hazelnuts

Hemp seeds
(½ cup)

Macadamia nuts

Pecans

Pistachios
(shelled)

Pepitas (pumpkin seeds)

Shredded coconut
(1½ cups)

Sunflower seeds

Walnuts

LIQUID

filtered water
(3 cups)

**SWEETNESS
(1–2 tablespoons)**

Brown rice syrup

Date(s), pitted

Pure maple syrup

**OPTIONAL
ADDITIONS
(1 teaspoon–
3 tablespoons)**

Cacao powder

Coconut butter

Coconut oil

Freshly grated
ginger

Freshly grated
nutmeg

Ground cinnamon

Ground turmeric
+ pinch freshly
ground black
pepper

Sesame seeds

BLACK SESAME WALNUT MILK

MAKES 3 CUPS

1 cup raw walnuts

3 tablespoons black sesame seeds

1–2 dates, pitted

6 cups filtered water

METHOD

Combine the walnuts, sesame seeds, and date(s) in a bowl. Cover with 3 cups of the filtered water and set aside at room temperature for at least 5 hours or overnight.

Rinse and drain, discarding the soaking liquid. Transfer the nuts, seeds, and dates to a blender and add the remaining 3 cups of filtered water. Blend until smooth.

Using a cheesecloth, nut milk bag, or an ultra-fine-mesh sieve, strain the nut milk, reserving the pulp. Transfer the milk to an airtight jar and store in the refrigerator for up to 5 days.

TO MAKE ICED PLANT MILK: Pour plant milk into a stainless steel ice cube tray or onto a small, rimmed baking sheet lined with parchment paper and freeze. If you choose the baking sheet option, it's perfect for milkshakes (page 85).

TO DRY THE PULP: Preheat the oven to 170°F. Evenly spread the pulp onto a parchment paper–lined baking sheet. Bake for 2 to 4 hours, turning the mixture occasionally to ensure even drying. When dry, process into a finely ground flour for baking and store in the freezer.

NOTE: If you don't have time to dry out the pulp, just spread it onto a parchment paper–lined baking sheet and freeze it.

ICED MILKSHAKES

This drink was always a childhood favorite of mine at the Hong Kong mom-and-pop diners known as *dai pai dong*. This recipe is a much healthier version, without refined sugars and condensed milk.

CHOOSE YOUR FAVORITE COMBINATION

LIQUID (½ cup)

Coffee

Filtered water

Plant Milk (page 82)

FROZEN (1 cup)

Ice

Plant Milk Ice (page 83)

Nice Cream (page 226; 1 cup)

SWEETNESS (1–2 teaspoons)

Brown rice syrup

Pitted dates

Pure maple syrup

FLAVOR (¼–½ cup)

Adzuki beans (cooked)

Bananas

Beets

Nut Butter (page 40)

Raw chocolate

Strawberries

CHUNKY EXTRAS

Adzuki beans (cooked)

Bliss Balls (page 218)

Brownies (page 228)

Cake (page 241)

Cookies (page 231)

Sweet potatoes (cooked)

ADDITIONAL FLAVOR (¼ teaspoon)

Cacao powder

Freshly grated ginger

Freshly grated nutmeg

Ground cinnamon

Ground turmeric (+ pinch freshly ground black pepper)

Mint extract

Vanilla extract

RED BEAN MILKSHAKE

MAKES 1 SERVING

¼ cup cooked adzuki beans

1 cup Coconut Milk Ice (page 83)

½ cup Cashew Milk (page 82)

¼ cup chopped beet

1 date, pitted

¼ teaspoon vanilla extract

1 tablespoon large coconut flakes for topping

METHOD

Spoon half of the adzuki beans into the bottom of the glass, reserving the rest for blending into the drink. Place most of the coconut milk ice in a blender (reserving a little for the top) and blend until smooth. Add the cashew milk, the remaining beans, the beet, the date, and the vanilla and blend again until smooth.

Transfer the contents of the blender into the glass. Top with the reserved coconut milk ice and the coconut flakes and serve.

SUPER SMOOTHIES

A smoothie or smoothie bowl is a perfect way to have a substantial liquid meal or snack that incorporates a rainbow of fruits and vegetables—any time of day. You can prepare smoothie packs in advance to keep in your freezer for easy grab 'n' blend convenience. Let your smoothie pack thaw a bit before blending; you may need to add more liquid to break up the frozen fruit. But if you want a thick, scoopable meal (that is, a smoothie bowl), don't use too much liquid. A Zoothie is a smoothie that uses zucchini as its base rather than bananas.

LIQUID BASE
(1–2 cups for smoothies; ¼–½ cup for smoothie bowls)

Coconut water

Filtered water

Freshly squeezed citrus juice

Nut Milk (page 82)

SWEETNESS
(1 piece / 1 tablespoon)

Brown rice syrup

Pitted date

Pure maple syrup

THICKENERS
(1 cup)

Avocados (frozen)

Bananas

Butternut squash

Cauliflower

Mangoes

Pumpkin

Sweet potatoes

Zucchini (cooked)

OTHER PRODUCE
(1 cup)

Beets

Berries

Carrots

Cherries

Citrus

Cranberries

Cucumbers

Kiwis

Mangoes

Peaches

Persimmons

Pineapple

LEAFY GREENS
(1 cup)

Beet greens

Bok choy

Cabbage (¼ cup)

Green leaf lettuce

Kale

Microgreens

Romaine

Spinach

PROTEIN/FATS
(1–2 tablespoons)

Chia seeds

Coconut oil

Dark chocolate

Hemp seeds

Nut Butter (page 40)

Nuts

Plant Milk Pulp (page 83)

OPTIONAL ADDITIONS
(½ teaspoon–1 tablespoon)

Cacao powder

Chilies

Freshly grated ginger

Fresh herbs

Freshly squeezed citrus juice and zest

SPICES

Ground turmeric

+

Freshly ground black pepper

PERSIMMON KUMQUAT ZOOTHIE BOWL

1 cup frozen yellow summer squash

1 persimmon, peeled and quartered

½ cup kumquats

¼ cup filtered water

¼ cup Napa cabbage

1 tablespoon pure maple syrup

1 tablespoon hemp seeds

1 teaspoon ground turmeric

¼ teaspoon freshly ground black pepper

METHOD

Combine all of the ingredients in a blender and blend until smooth. Serve with a variety of fresh fruits and toppings.

TIP: To avoid the danger of a smoothie that looks like sludge, try using fruits and vegetables that are the same color.

KOMBUCHA

The process of brewing your own kombucha might seem daunting, but it's actually pretty straightforward and fun to brew your own flavors. You just need time and patience to let nature—in the form of a SCOBY (symbiotic colony of bacteria and yeast)—digest the sugars for you. I noted earlier that plastics are often used in the production of tea bags, so I recommend loose-leaf tea as a 100-percent compostable, zero-waste option. Loose-leaf teas generally come in tins; some are sold in bulk food stores.

CHOOSE YOUR FAVORITE COMBINATION

KOMBUCHA BASE
(12 ounces)

A) UNFLAVORED
(1 teaspoon)

Coconut sugar
Pure maple syrup
Raw organic cane sugar

B) FLAVORED WITH
FRESH FRUIT JUICE
(1 teaspoon)

Apple
Beets
Berries
Carrots
Cherries

Citrus
Cranberries
Freshly grated ginger
Grapefruit
Grapes
Kiwis
Mangoes
Oranges
Peaches
Pineapple

C) FLAVORED WITH
INGREDIENTS, CHOPPED
(1 tablespoon)

Berries
Cherries

Citrus
Cranberries
Freshly grated ginger
Kiwis
Mangoes
Peaches
Pineapple

D) OPTIONAL INFUSIONS

Cloves
Fresh basil
Lavender
Lemongrass
Mint
Vanilla bean (split)

FIRST FERMENT

White vinegar for sanitizing
8 cups filtered water
1 cup raw organic cane sugar

4 tablespoons loose-leaf green or
   black tea leaves
1 cup kombucha
1 SCOBY

METHOD

First, sanitize all of your equipment by cleaning it thoroughly. Add a splash of the white vinegar to a heatproof jar. Seal the jar and shake vigorously until frothy. Rinse with boiling water and then set aside to air dry.

Bring 2 cups of the filtered water to a boil and pour it into a teapot. Add the sugar and tea leaves and stir until the sugar dissolves. Set aside to steep for 10 minutes.

Strain the sweetened tea into the prepared jar and compost the tea leaves. Add the rest of the water to the jar and set aside to cool completely.

Carefully wash your hands using a fragrance-free bar soap (be sure not to use hand sanitizer or antibacterial soap, as they will harm the bacteria in the SCOBY) and make sure there is no soap residue on your hands. Add the kombucha and SCOBY to the jar.

Cover the jar with cheesecloth or a linen napkin and secure it with a rubber band or string. Set aside to ferment in a cool, dark, and well-ventilated spot for 7 to 12 days; try not to move the jar.

After 7 days, use a ceramic or wooden spoon to taste for sweetness; if it's too sweet, keep fermenting for another day or two (the cooler the temperature, the longer it will take to ferment, and the longer it ferments, the less sweet it will be).

During the fermentation process, a new SCOBY will form. Remove the mother and baby SCOBY, along with 1 cup of the kombucha to make another batch. Store the kombucha for the next batch in an airtight jar in a cool, dark place.

Divide the rest of the first-ferment brew into 12-ounce bottles, leaving 2-inches of air space from the top of each, for the second fermentation process. The second ferment promotes carbonation.

SECOND FERMENT: A, B, C, OR D (PER 12 OUNCES)

METHOD

Add the desired additions from A, B, or C (plus something from D if desired) to each bottle and tightly cover the bottles. Store at room temperature for 2 to 5 days; open the lid of each bottle once a day to release the gases and "burp" them, so they don't explode.

Drink ¼-cup shots of the kombucha throughout the day before meals and after dinner to aid in digestion.

NOTE: A SCOBY should never be moldy or mushy or have dark spots. It should be a whitish color and should feel like fresh calamari. Store your SCOBY with 1 cup kombucha in an airtight jar in a cool, dark (but not refrigerated) place. The more often you brew your own kombucha, the more SCOBY babies you will have. Gift these in glass jars to friends or family so they can join in on the fun too!

CONCORD GRAPE

24 ounces First-Ferment Kombucha (page 88)

2 teaspoons Concord grape juice

SOUR CHERRY AND CRANBERRY

24 ounces First-Ferment Kombucha (page 88)

1 teaspoon sour cherry juice

1 tablespoon cranberries

LEMONGRASS GINGER

24 ounces First-Ferment Kombucha (page 88)

1 tablespoon freshly grated ginger

1 fresh lemongrass stem

GREEN JUICE

A fresh green juice or smoothie either first thing in the morning or before a meal will give your body a natural boost and plenty of health benefits. This flood of raw nutrition—in the form of highly concentrated vitamins, minerals, and enzymes—quickly enters the bloodstream and allows your body to maximize all of the nutritional benefits. By drinking the juice and skipping the fiber, you're also letting your gut temporarily rest and repair. Keeping a ratio of 80 percent vegetables to 20 percent fruit helps you avoid blood sugar spikes and helps maintain satiety. Making your own green juice gives you flexibility in taste and the benefit of optimal nutritional value, and it's more cost effective, too! If you don't have a juicer, blend the ingredients together and strain out the pulp, just as you would with nut milk.

CHOOSE YOUR FAVORITE COMBINATION

BASE (3 cups)

Apples

Carrots

Cucumbers

Pineapple

Watermelon

VEGETABLES (1–2 pieces)

Beets

Celery

Fennel

LEAFY (4 cups)

Chard

Collards

Kale

Lettuce

Spinach

FRUIT (1–2 pieces)

Apples

Berries

Grapefruit

Grapes

Kiwis

Lemons

Mangoes

Oranges

Pears

ADDITIONS (¼ cup chopped)

Fresh basil

Fresh cilantro

Freshly grated ginger

Fresh mint

Jalapeño peppers

ROMAINE HOLIDAY

MAKES 2 SERVINGS (3 CUPS)

4 cups romaine lettuce, roughly chopped

2 green apples, peeled and roughly chopped

1 zucchini, peeled and roughly chopped

1 cup spinach, roughly chopped

¼ cup roughly chopped fresh basil

1 celery stalk, roughly chopped

½ lime, peeled and roughly chopped

METHOD

Extract the ingredients through a juicer. Serve.

SAVORY BLENDS

Savory blends are really just smoothies without fruit. On the plane rides home to Hong Kong during holiday breaks in my college years, I'd often order a V8 vegetable and fruit drink for a good in-flight vitamin boost during those long-haul trips. Spicy drinks stimulate blood circulation and digestion.

CHOOSE YOUR FAVORITE COMBINATION

BASE (1–2 cups)

Cucumbers

Filtered water

Tomatoes

Watermelon

FLAVORS (½ cup)

Beets

Carrots

Celery

Cucumbers

PROTEIN/FATS (1–2 tablespoons)

Beans (cooked)

Chia seeds

Hemp seeds

THICKENERS (1 cup)

Avocados (frozen)

Butternut squash

Cauliflower

Pumpkin

Sweet potatoes

Zucchini (cooked)

LEAFY (1 cup)

Cabbage (½ cup)

Kale

Romaine

Spinach

Sweet potato leaves

ADDITIONS (½ teaspoon–1 tablespoon)

Chili peppers

Fresh herbs

Freshly grated ginger

Garlic

Onion

Salt + freshly ground black pepper

Spices

SPICY MARY

MAKES 1 SERVING

3 tomatoes

1 cup cooked butternut squash

1 cup romaine lettuce

2 celery stalks

1 red chili pepper

1 tablespoon hemp seeds

½ golden beet, thinly sliced

Salt to taste

Freshly ground black pepper
to taste

METHOD

Combine the tomatoes, butternut squash, romaine lettuce, 1 of the celery stalks, the chili pepper, hemp seeds, and almost all of the beet slices in a blender and blend until smooth. Season with the salt and black pepper and serve, garnished with the remaining celery stalk and beet slices.

SNACKS

Opposite: Hummus, page 98, and Seeded Crackers, page 102

HUMMUS

Hummus is another staple that tastes tremendously better when you make it from scratch. Whenever I make this and bring it to parties, people are always surprised at how flavorful it is compared to store-bought counterparts. The best thing is that you can incorporate unique flavors, and sometimes festive colors, by adding a variety of fresh ingredients, like sunchokes, carrots, or beets.

CHOOSE YOUR FAVORITE COMBINATION

**BASE
(2 cups, cooked)**

Cannellini beans

Chickpeas

Lentils (red or yellow)

Lima beans

Navy beans

FATS (¼ cup)

Olive oil

Tahini

Unsweetened Nut Butter (page 40)

FLAVORS (1 cup)

Artichoke hearts

Beets

Carrots

Edamame

Fresh herbs

Roasted red peppers

Spinach

Sunchokes (cooked)

Sweet potatoes (cooked)

or (¼ cup)

Olives

Sun-dried tomatoes

**ACIDITY
(2 tablespoons)**

Apple cider vinegar

Freshly squeezed lemon juice

LIQUID (¼ cup or less)

Filtered water

Freshly squeezed orange juice

**SEASONINGS
(1–2 teaspoons)**

Ground cumin

+

¾ teaspoon salt

+

¼ teaspoon freshly ground black pepper

+

1–2 garlic cloves, minced

CARROT RED LENTIL HUMMUS

1 cup red lentils

2 cups filtered water

2 carrots, chopped

2 tablespoons freshly squeezed lemon juice

2 tablespoons olive oil, plus more for drizzling

2 tablespoons tahini

2 garlic cloves, minced

1 teaspoon ground cumin

¾ teaspoon salt

¼ teaspoon freshly ground black pepper

¼ cup freshly squeezed orange juice or as needed for consistency

Pinch chili powder for sprinkling

METHOD

Rinse the lentils. Place them in a stockpot over high heat with the water and carrots and bring to a boil. Reduce the heat to low, cover, and simmer for 18 to 20 minutes until all the water is absorbed. Remove from the heat, drain, and set aside to cool.

In a food processor fitted with the "S" blade, combine the lentils, the carrots, the lemon juice, the olive oil, the tahini, the garlic, the cumin, the salt, and the black pepper and puree. As the machine is running, add the orange juice, 1 tablespoon at a time, until you reach the desired consistency (you may not need all the liquid, as it may get too runny). Taste and adjust the flavors as necessary by adding more olive oil, cumin, salt, or lemon juice.

Transfer to a serving bowl, drizzle with the olive oil, and sprinkle with the chili powder. Serve with any garnishes you like.

VEGAN CHEESE

Cheese is one of the most difficult things to substitute when opting for a dairy-free or vegan diet. Who would have thought that after you soak and blend nuts, they're truly creamy. Nutritional yeast (aka "nooch"), an inactive yeast grown on molasses, is a fungus that's dried with heat and imparts lots of cheesy flavor and richness. It's a good source of vitamin B12, folic acid, zinc, and protein.

CHOOSE YOUR FAVORITE COMBINATION

NUTS (1½ cups, soaked and drained)	LIQUID TO BLEND	SEASONINGS (½ teaspoon)
Almonds	Filtered water (2–4 tablespoons)	Garlic
Brazil nuts	+	Nutritional yeast
Cashews	Freshly squeezed lemon juice (2 tablespoons)	Salt
Hazelnuts		Spices
Macadamia nuts	FERMENTATION	(2 tablespoons) to coat
Pecans	1–2 probiotic capsules	Fresh chives
Pistachios (shelled)	or	Fresh herbs
Walnuts	1 teaspoon miso paste	Freshly ground black pepper

BRAZIL NUT CHEESE

1 cup Brazil nuts, soaked overnight and drained

2 tablespoons freshly squeezed lemon juice

2 tablespoons nutritional yeast

2 tablespoons filtered water

1 teaspoon miso paste

½ teaspoon salt

Freshly ground black pepper for coating

METHOD

In a food processor fitted with the "S" blade or a blender, combine the brazil nuts, lemon juice, nutritional yeast, water, miso paste, and salt. Blend until smooth and thick, like a paste. Use as little of the water as possible—just enough to make the mixture creamy.

Serve immediately as a delicious spread or age it (see note). If aging the cheese, grind the pepper onto a small plate. Press the cheese onto the black pepper until evenly coated. Refrigerate until ready to use.

NOTE: If you want to age the cheese, form the mixture into a ball and wrap completely in cheesecloth or line a small bowl or dish with cheesecloth and press the spread into it, creating a firm shape. Wrap it up and set aside to rest overnight at room temperature.

SEEDED CRACKERS

My lovely neighbor introduced me to this hearty Norwegian cracker recipe. The seedy goodness packs a punch, and they're deliciously addictive. You can either break these sheets up into rustic pieces, or, using a sharp knife, cut them into squares or rectangles right after you pull them out of the oven.

CHOOSE YOUR FAVORITE COMBINATION

BASE	FLOUR (½ cup)	LARGE SEEDS
Rolled oats (1 cup)	Brown rice flour	Pepitas (pumpkin seeds)
+	Nut Flour (page 83)	Sunflower
Flax seeds (¼ cup)	Oat flour (ground up oats)	**SMALL SEEDS**
+	Spelt flour	Poppy seeds
1 teaspoon salt	Whole wheat flour	Sesame seeds
		LIQUID (1⅔ cup)
		Filtered water

PUMPKIN AND POPPYSEED CRACKERS

MAKES 2 (13-BY-7-INCH) TRAYS

1⅔ cups filtered water
1 cup gluten-free oats
½ cup brown rice flour
½ cup pumpkin seeds

¼ cup sesame seeds
¼ cup flax seeds
1 teaspoon salt

METHOD

Preheat the oven to 400°F. Line two baking sheets with parchment paper.

In a large bowl, stir together all of the ingredients. Set aside for 10 to 15 minutes.

Dollop small spoonfuls of the batter 2 inches apart directly on one of the prepared baking sheets. Wet your fingertips with warm water and gently pat down each spoonful until it has been spread across the entire sheet in an even layer, without any gaps or holes. Repeat with the other baking sheet.

Bake for 22 to 25 minutes, switching the baking sheets from the top to bottom racks (and front to back) after 10 minutes (I also like to peel them off the parchment paper and flip them over so the bottoms are evenly crisped). The crackers are done when

they are lightly golden and crisp; the center generally takes longer to cook, so if the center is not done but the edges are crisp, remove the edge pieces. Return the baking sheet to the oven and turn off the heat, using the cool-down time to finish off the centers. Remove from the oven and set aside to cool completely.

Store in an airtight tin or a glass jar for 10 days.

TRAIL MIX

Trail mix is so easy to customize to your own taste that it makes no sense to buy a pre-packaged mix. You can find all the ingredients you need in the bulk-food section of the supermarket and take them home in your own containers to create your favorite combination. I love to make a big batch of this for holiday gifts. They're a good staple to prepare in advance for a substantial snack anytime or to add crunch to a salad. If you enjoy a bit of sweetness, add some chopped dried fruits to the mix.

RAW NUTS + SEEDS (1 pound)	OIL (1 tablespoon)	Curry powder	OPTIONAL DRIED FRUIT ADDITIONS (½ cup)
Almonds	Coconut	Five-spice powder	Apples
Brazil nuts	Olive	Freshly ground black pepper	Apricots
Cashews	Sesame, light	Garlic powder	Banana chips
Hazelnuts	Sunflower seed	Ground cinnamon	Cranberries
Macadamia nuts	+	Ground cumin	Coconut
Pecans	SWEET (1 tablespoon)	Ground mustard	Figs
Pepitas (pumpkin seeds)	Brown rice syrup	Powdered ginger	Goji berries
Pistachios (shelled)	Coconut sugar	Onion powder	Mangoes
Sunflower seeds	Pure maple syrup	Smoked paprika	Pineapple
Walnuts	Raw cane sugar		Prunes
		FRESH (2 tablespoons)	Raisins
SALT (½ teaspoon)	SEASONINGS (¼ teaspoon– 1 tablespoon)	Garlic	
Salt	Balsamic vinegar	Freshly squeezed citrus juice	
Tamari or soy sauce	Cayenne pepper	Fresh oregano	
	Cocoa powder	Fresh rosemary	
		Fresh thyme	

CURRY LIME TRAIL MIX

MAKES 10 TO 12 SERVINGS

1 tablespoon coconut oil	2 teaspoons curry powder
2 cups mixed nuts	¼ teaspoon cayenne pepper
2 garlic cloves, minced	½ teaspoon salt
1 tablespoon pure maple syrup	Squeeze of fresh lime juice

METHOD

In a cast-iron skillet over medium-high heat, warm the coconut oil. Reduce the heat to medium and add the nuts, tossing until well coated. Continue toasting the nuts for 5 to 7 minutes, stirring frequently to ensure even toasting and to prevent burning.

Stir in the remaining ingredients until well combined and continue to toast for 1 more minute. Remove from the heat and transfer to a cooling rack lined with parchment paper to cool. There's nothing more comfortingly addictive than freshly roasted nuts, but if you have any left, set aside to cool completely before storing in an airtight container.

VEGGIE CHIPS

I've always been a big snacker, but a couple of recent incidents ended my procrastination habit of picking up a bag of potato chips or other crunchy snacks. First, I underwent a food allergy test that tested positive for potatoes, and second, I committed myself to not purchase products that come in single-use packaging. Homemade chips are easy and versatile—and so much better for you, without all the excess oil! This recipe is another three-ingredient favorite.

CHOOSE YOUR FAVORITE COMBINATION

VEGETABLES (1–2 pieces)

Beets

Kabocha squash

Lotus root

Parsnips

Plantains

Potatoes

Sunchokes

Sweet potatoes

Taro root

OIL (1 tablespoon)

Coconut

Olive

Sesame, light

Sunflower seed

SEASONING (to taste)

Chili pepper

Curry powder

Dried oregano

Garlic powder

Ground turmeric

Onion powder

Paprika, sweet or smoked

Nutritional yeast

Salt

Za'atar

PARSNIP CHIPS

MAKES 2 TO 4 SERVINGS

3 large parsnips

2 tablespoons olive oil

1 teaspoon garlic powder, plus more if needed

½ teaspoon salt, plus more if needed

METHOD

Preheat the oven to 250°F.

Scrub or peel the parsnips. Using a mandoline, evenly and thinly cut the parsnips into ⅛-inch-thick (or thinner) slices.

Pour the olive oil into a bowl and add the parsnips. Using your fingertips, evenly coat each slice with a thin layer of oil.

Arrange the slices in single layers on the baking sheets without overlapping the pieces. Lightly season with the garlic powder and salt.

Bake for 60 to 70 minutes, or until crisp, rotating the baking sheets after 35 minutes (top to bottom, front to back). If the chips are only slightly soft at the end of the baking time, they will crisp up as they cool, but if the pieces are "bendy," return to the oven for 5 to 10 more minutes. Remove from the oven.

Taste and reseason with the garlic powder and salt if desired. Serve or set aside to cool completely on the baking sheets and then store in an airtight container (if you have any left!) for up to 3 days.

VARIATION: You can also bake these at 400°F for 15 to 17 minutes, but keep an eye on them for the last few minutes and take out any pieces that have already crisped and turned slightly golden first—they can burn and turn quite bitter in a matter of seconds at the end. If pieces are still very soft, flip them over and return to the oven for 1 to 3 more minutes.

TOAST

After eating a plain piece of toast, I'm usually hungry within an hour. Although bread is certainly convenient to reach for when you're looking for something to eat, empty carbs aren't the best way to satisfy yourself, nutritionally speaking. These sweet potato slices are naturally Paleo and gluten-free. They make the perfect vehicle for yummy toppings without spiking your blood sugar. A little creamy element will keep the toppings from falling off.

CHOOSE YOUR FAVORITE COMBINATION

BASE

Bagel

Essential Loaf
(page 73)

Flatbreads
(page 168)

Flour Tortillas
(page 174)

Seeded Crackers
(page 102)

Sourdough

Sweet Potato
Toasts (recipe
follows)

CREAMINESS

Cashewgurt
(page 46)

Chutney (page 131)

Hummus (page 98)

Nut Cheese
(page 101)

Oil-Free
Mayonnaise
(page 62)

Roasted Eggplant
Dip (page 170)

TOPPINGS

Avocados

Carrot Lox
(page 65)

Cucumbers

Hummus (page 98)

Jalapeño peppers

Microgreens

Mushroom
Tapenade (recipe
follows)

Radishes

Red onion

Roasted Eggplant
Dip (page 170)

Tomato

Tomatuna
(page 142)

SWEET POTATO TOASTS

1 large sweet potato

2 teaspoons olive oil

¼ teaspoon salt

METHOD

Wash and peel the sweet potato and cut it into ¼-inch slices.

In a cast-iron skillet over medium-high heat, warm the olive oil. Add the sweet potato slices and fry for 3 to 5 minutes on each side, or until blistered and crisp. Remove from the heat.

The toasts are best served warm with the toppings of your choice.

MUSHROOM TAPENADE

1 tablespoon olive oil

1 shallot, finely chopped

1 garlic clove, minced

8 ounces mushrooms, chopped

¼ cup pitted olives, chopped

1 tablespoon fresh oregano

1 teaspoon apple cider vinegar

½ teaspoon salt

METHOD

In a cast-iron skillet over medium-high heat, warm the olive oil. Add the shallot and garlic and sauté for 2 minutes, or until softened. Add the mushrooms and continue to sauté for 5 more minutes. Remove from the heat, add the remaining ingredients, and toss until well combined.

Spoon generously onto the toast of your choice and serve.

ONIGIRI (RICE BALLS)

A traditional Japanese version of fast food, these rice balls are seasoned and sometimes stuffed with a filling for a tasty breakfast or snack.

CHOOSE YOUR FAVORITE COMBINATION

RICE (2 cups)

Purple sticky

Short-grain brown

Short-grain white

ADDITIONS

1 tablespoon rice vinegar

+

½ teaspoon salt

WRAP (OPTIONAL)

Nori seaweed strips

Perilla/shiso leaves

FILLING (8 teaspoons)

Adzuki beans (cooked)

Carrot Lox (page 65)

Mock "Tuna" Salad
(page 61)

Mushroom Tapenade
(page 109)

Pekingbello (page 145)

Pickles (page 151)

Tomatuna (page 142)

CARROT ONIGIRI

MAKES 8

1 cup short-grain white rice

1 cup short-grain brown rice

3½ cups filtered water

1 carrot, finely chopped

1 or 2 chard leaves, finely chopped

1 tablespoon rice vinegar

½ teaspoon salt

3 tablespoons sesame seeds

METHOD

Combine the rice varieties in a fine-mesh sieve and rinse well. Drain and transfer to a saucepan with a tight-fitting lid.

Add the water and place over high heat. Bring to a boil. Cover immediately, reduce the heat to low, and simmer for 20 to 30 minutes, or until all the liquid is absorbed. Remove from the heat.

Stir in the chopped carrot, chard leaves, rice vinegar, and salt. Cover with a dish towel and set aside to cool slightly (it will be warm but not too hot to handle).

Wet your hands with warm water to keep the rice from sticking to them. Place a scant ½ cup of the mixture in the palm of your hand and slightly flatten it. Firmly press until a tight ball forms. Gently roll the ball in the sesame seeds and transfer to a plate. Continue with the remaining mixture until all of it has been used.

SAVORY

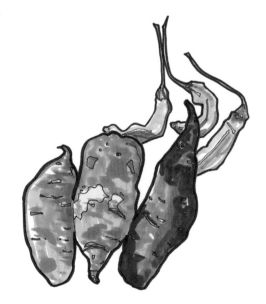

SENSATIONAL SALADS

A salad doesn't need to be just plain lettuce leaves and a dressing. Think about adding MORE to these leaves to create a colorful meal with a combination of textures and flavors that can also change with the seasons. Combine raw vegetables with cooked ones for variety, and always add protein to make this a nutritionally balanced and substantial meal. Using leftovers is also a great way to put a unique salad together.

CHOOSE YOUR FAVORITE COMBINATION

LEAFY GREENS (1 to 2 cups)	VEGETABLES (½ cup × 1 or 2, raw)	VEGETABLES (½ cup × 1 or 2, cooked)	FRUIT (OPTIONAL; ½ cup)
Arugula	Arugula	Artichokes	Apples
Cabbage	Asparagus	Asparagus	Berries
Lettuce	Avocados	Bok choy	Citrus
Kale	Beets	Broccoli	Figs
Radicchio	Broccoli	Brussels sprouts	Grapefruit
Spinach	Brussels sprouts	Butternut squash	Grapes
Watercress	Carrots	Cauliflower	Mangoes
PROTEIN (½ cup)	Cauliflower	Corn	Peaches
SEE TABLE ABOVE	Celery	Eggplant	Pears
	Cucumbers	Fennel	Pomegranate arils
HEALTHY FATS (¼ cup)	Fennel	Green beans	Tomatoes
Avocados	Green beans	Mushrooms	
Nuts	Kale	Okra	**CARBOHYDRATES, OPTIONAL (1 cup)**
Seeds	Kohlrabi	Parsnips	
Salad Dressing (page 116; 1 tablespoon)	Lettuce	Peppers	Millet
	Peppers	Potatoes	Potatoes
	Radishes	Pumpkin	Wild rice
	Snap peas	Romanesco	
	Sprouts (page 24)	Sweet potatoes	
	Tomatoes	Turnips	
	Zucchini	Zucchini	

ASIAN PEAR SALAD

MAKES 1 SERVING

2 cups kale

1 teaspoon olive oil

1 carrot, julienned

½ cup cooked chickpeas
    (page 26)

½ Asian pear, thinly sliced

Chili powder to taste

1 tablespoon Black Pepper
    Dressing (page 117)

METHOD

Prepare the kale by removing the leafy bits from the stems (save the stems for the Root-to-Leaf Stock on page 215). Tear into bite-size pieces. Using your fingertips, massage the olive oil into the leaves and place them in a serving bowl.

Add the carrot, chickpeas, and pear slices to the bowl and toss. Sprinkle with the chili powder, dress with the black pepper dressing, and serve.

DRESSING

CHOOSE YOUR FAVORITE COMBINATION

OIL (¼ cup)

Avocado

Nut

Olive

Sesame, light

+

¼ teaspoon salt

HERBS (1 tablespoon chopped)

Fresh basil

Fresh chives

Fresh oregano

Fresh parsley

Fresh rosemary

ACIDITY (1 tablespoon)

Apple cider vinegar

Balsamic vinegar

Freshly squeezed lemon juice

Freshly squeezed lime juice

Freshly squeezed orange juice

Red wine vinegar

Rice vinegar

White wine vinegar

OPTIONAL FLAVORS (2 tablespoons to ¼ cup)

Avocados

Carrots

Mangoes

Nut Butter (page 40)

Raspberries

Roasted garlic

Tahini

SEASONING (½–1 teaspoon)

Chili flakes

Curry powder

Freshly ground black pepper

Garlic powder

Ground ginger

Mustard

Nutritional yeast

Tamari or soy sauce

Toasted sesame oil

BLACK PEPPER DRESSING

¼ cup walnut oil

1 tablespoon freshly squeezed
blood orange juice

1 tablespoon finely chopped fresh
cilantro

1 teaspoon freshly ground black
pepper

¼ teaspoon salt

METHOD

Just before you are ready to dress a salad, whisk together all of the ingredients in a
small bowl until the dressing emulsifies. Drizzle onto the salad and toss. Serve.

NOTE: Some dressings might need thinning out when you add the optional flavors. Blend
your dressing with ¼ to ⅓ cup filtered water, depending on how thick you want it to be.

CREAMY SOUPS

Cauliflower puree provides a creamy texture to dishes, and because of its white color, you can add (or sneak) it into just about any soup to add some nutritional value. In this recipe, I add white beans to boost the amount of the soup's protein and to balance out the flavors of the celery and parsnip. I like to reserve a few tablespoons of the fresh vegetables in the soup and sprinkle them on as a garnish; it also provides a little texture to complement the soup's creaminess.

CHOOSE YOUR FAVORITE COMBINATION

OIL (2 tablespoons)

Coconut

Olive

Sesame, light

Sunflower seed

AROMATICS (½ cup)

Fresh chives

Freshly grated ginger

Garlic

Green onion

Leeks

Onion

Shallots

SEASONING (to taste)

Freshly ground black pepper

Nutritional yeast

Salt

CREAMINESS (1 cup)

Cauliflower florets

Coconut Milk (page 82)

+

(½ cup)

Pulses (cooked; page 26)

Raw cashews

VEGETABLES (1 pound)

Beets

Butternut squash

Carrots

Celery

Corn

Mushrooms

Parsnips

Peas + broccoli

Potatoes + leeks

Pumpkin

Sweet potatoes

LIQUID (2–3 cups)

Coconut Milk (page 82)

Filtered water

Root-to-Leaf Stock (page 215)

SPRINKLES

Chili flakes

Dukkah

Fresh chives

Fresh herbs

Freshly ground black pepper

Freshly squeezed citrus juice and zest

Green onions

Hemp seeds

Microgreens

Sesame seeds

Sprouts (page 24)

Here are some creamy soup creations (a.k.a. not a smoothie) by:

ROW 1: @picturethatfood @appalachianofferings @thelittleplantation
ROW 2: @eatsleepgreen @cupcakeree @shisodelicious
ROW 3: @curlew_and_dragonfly @foodiegudi @nourish_deliciously

More inspiration can be found on Instagram #notasmoothieparty

CELERY, PARSNIP, AND WHITE BEAN SOUP

MAKES 3 TO 4 SERVINGS

2 tablespoons olive oil

½ onion, chopped

2 parsnips, chopped

3 celery stalks, chopped

1 cup chopped cauliflower florets

½ cup cooked navy beans

2 cups filtered water, plus more as needed

½ teaspoon salt, plus more to taste

METHOD

In a large stockpot over medium heat, warm the olive oil. Add the onion and sauté for 3 to 5 minutes. Add the parsnips, celery, cauliflower, and navy beans and toss until well combined.

Add the 2 cups of water and the ½ teaspoon of the salt to the stockpot and bring to a boil. Reduce the heat to low, cover, and simmer for 10 to 15 minutes, or until the vegetables are soft. Remove from the heat.

Blend or process the soup and add a little more of the water, if necessary, to get the soup to the desired consistency.

Taste and season further with the salt if necessary. Return the stockpot to low heat and warm for 5 minutes. Remove from the heat and serve.

CHILLED SOUPS

In the summer, when it's way too hot to cook, a gazpacho can be a refreshing change of pace. I find that adding watermelon means extra thirst-quenching value. Peel the cucumber and zucchini if you prefer your soup to look vibrant, colorful, and refreshing. Reserve some of the finely chopped ingredients for garnishes, or add other ingredients to complement the flavors.

CHOOSE YOUR FAVORITE COMBINATION

TOMATO BASE (4–5 pieces)	ADDITIONS (1–2 cups)	GARNISHES	LIQUID (½ cup or more, if necessary)
Plum	Avocados	Avocados	Ice-cold filtered water
Roma	Beets	Bell pepper	
Yellow	Bell peppers	Cucumbers	
	Cucumbers	Fresh basil	SEASONING (to taste)
AROMATICS	Leafy greens	Fresh cilantro	
⅛ onion	Microgreens	Fresh dill	Freshly ground black pepper
+	Peaches	Fresh mint	Salt
⅛ clove garlic	Summer squash	Peaches	
	Watermelon	Red onion	
	Zucchini	Summer squash	
		Tomatoes	
		Watermelon	
		Zucchini	

WATERMELON GAZPACHO

MAKES 2 TO 4 SERVINGS

3 tomatoes, roughly chopped
1 cup cubed watermelon
1 small zucchini, peeled
1 (6-inch) cucumber, peeled
⅛ onion

⅛ clove garlic
½ teaspoon salt
½ cup ice-cold filtered water or as needed

METHOD

In a blender or food processor fitted with the "S" blade, combine all of the ingredients except the water. Puree until the mixture is well blended and becomes a thick liquid. As the blender or food processor is running, gradually add the ice-cold water until it thins to the desired consistency.

Place a fine sieve over a bowl and pour the mixture into the sieve, pushing the pulp through to strain (depending on the power of your blender, you may or may not need to do this).

Transfer the filtered soup into a glass pitcher or jug and chill for 3 hours, or until ready to serve.

SANDWICHES

I'm not really much of a sandwich person. I prefer open-faced toast, but when I need to pack an easy on-the-go lunch, I grab whatever is in the refrigerator and stuff it in bread. Fresh loaves of bread and other baked goods can usually be purchased package-free, using your own bag or a recycled paper bag. Microgreens are small-but-mighty sprouts that contain anywhere from 4 to 40 times more nutritional value than their full-grown counterparts. They are also easy to grow at home, no matter where you live.

CHOOSE YOUR FAVORITE COMBINATION

BREAD (2 slices per person)

Bagel
Essential Loaf (page 73)
Flatbreads (page 168)
Sourdough

FILLING (½ cup)

Carrot Lox (page 65)
Falafel (page 132)
Frittata (page 69)
Hummus (page 98)
Pekingbello (page 145)

Roasted or Grilled Vegetables (page 210)
Veggie Burgers (page 135)

VEGETABLES (8 ounces)

Artichoke hearts
Cabbage
Leafy greens
Mushrooms
Radishes
Sprouts (page 24)
Sun-dried tomatoes
Tomatoes

CONDIMENTS

Cashew Cheese (page 101)
Chutney (page 131)
Kimchi (page 153)
Oil-Free Mayonnaise (page 62)
Pesto (page 164)
Pickles (page 151)
Roasted Eggplant Dip (page 170)

ROASTED BUTTERNUT SQUASH

MAKES 2 SERVINGS

1 butternut squash
2 tablespoons olive oil
1 teaspoon sweet paprika
Salt to taste
Freshly ground black pepper to taste
4 slices sourdough bread

Oil-Free Mayonnaise (page 62) to taste
Homemade Harissa (recipe follows) to taste
3 artichoke hearts, sliced
¼ cup sunflower microgreens
¼ cup red chard microgreens
1 radish, sliced

(continued)

METHOD

Preheat the oven to 425°F.

Cut the top section of the butternut squash into ½-inch rounds. You can peel the squash if you like, although it isn't necessary. Save the "bowl" segment of the squash for a stuffed dish (page 192).

Brush both sides of the butternut squash rounds with the olive oil and place them on a baking sheet. Season with the paprika, salt, and black pepper. Roast for 25 to 30 minutes, turning them once. Remove from the oven and set aside to cool for 10 minutes before preparing your sandwich.

Toast the bread, if desired.

Slather the oil-free mayonnaise on one side of one slice of the bread and the homemade harissa on the other slice. Stuff and layer your sandwich with the squash, artichoke hearts, microgreens, and radish slices and serve.

HOMEMADE HARISSA

MAKES 1 CUP

1 whole red bell pepper

1 teaspoon caraway seeds

1 teaspoon coriander seeds

1 teaspoon cumin seeds

3 fresh red chili peppers

3 garlic cloves

3 sun-dried tomatoes

3 tablespoons olive oil

2 tablespoons freshly squeezed
   lemon juice

½ teaspoon salt

METHOD

Roast the bell pepper directly over the flame of your stove's burner, charring the skin evenly. Wrap it in a dish towel and set aside.

Place a small, dry frying pan over medium-high heat. Add the caraway, coriander, and cumin seeds and toast for 2 to 3 minutes, or until lightly toasted and fragrant. Remove from the heat.

Transfer the seeds to a mortar and pestle and crush them thoroughly.

Peel the charred skin off the pepper and remove and discard the seeds.

In a high-speed blender or food processor fitted with the "S" blade, blend together all the ingredients.

Serve or transfer to an airtight glass jar and store in the refrigerator.

EMPANADAS

Handy pocket foods are another favorite for my family. The Chinese bao (bun), the Indian samosa, and the South American empanada are among those I've made at home. When my kids were younger, we often went to a family-run Argentinian restaurant in the neighborhood that specialized in these pocket meals. After it closed, we couldn't find a suitable replacement, so I ventured into making my own. To this day, they're a favorite for packed lunches. Because these are filled with cooked food, you can also stuff them with leftovers, such as Chili (page 201), Gratin (page 189), or Ratatian (page 185).

CHOOSE YOUR FAVORITE COMBINATION

DOUGH	SEASONINGS	VEGETABLES (1 cup)
(1 portion)	1 teaspoon ground cumin	Corn
	+	Mushrooms
BASE	1 teaspoon sweet paprika	Olives
1 tablespoon olive oil	+	Potatoes (cooked)
+	1 teaspoon dried oregano	Pumpkin (cooked)
1 shallot (finely chopped)	+	Sweet potatoes (cooked)
+	1 tablespoon chickpea (gram) or rice flour	**LEAFY GREENS (2 cups)**
1 tomato (finely chopped)	+	Cabbage
PROTEIN (1 cup)	½ teaspoon salt	Chard
Pulses (cooked; page 26)		Kale
Tofu		Spinach

BLACK BEAN AND CHARD EMPANADAS

MAKES 4 TO 6

FOR THE FILLING

1 tablespoon olive oil

1 shallot, finely chopped

2 portobello mushrooms, finely chopped

1 cup cooked black beans (page 26)

1 tomato, finely chopped

1 tablespoon chickpea (gram) or rice flour

1 teaspoon ground cumin

1 teaspoon sweet paprika

1 teaspoon dried oregano

½ teaspoon salt

2 cups rainbow chard, stems removed and shredded

(continued)

1 cup spelt flour

½ cup buckwheat flour

1 tablespoon flax seed meal

½ teaspoon salt

3 tablespoons vegan butter, cold

½ cup ice-cold filtered water or
more as needed

Olive oil for brushing

Spiced Pear Chutney (page 131)
for serving

METHOD

Make the filling: In a saucepan over high heat, warm the olive oil. Add the shallot and sauté for 3 to 5 minutes, or until softened and fragrant. Stir in the remaining ingredients except the chard until evenly combined and cook for 7 more minutes.

Add the chard and remove from the heat. Set aside to cool while preparing the dough.

Make the dough: Preheat the oven to 400°F. Line a baking sheet with parchment paper.

In a food processor fitted with the "S" blade, combine the flours, flax seed meal, and salt and process until very well combined. Add the vegan butter and pulse a few times, just until the mixture resembles small crumbs. Add the cold water 1 teaspoon at a time, pulsing as you go, just until the moment the dough forms into a ball.

Turn out the dough onto a well-floured work surface and knead with your hands for 2 to 3 minutes. Form the dough into four to six equal balls. Roll each ball out to a ¼-inch thickness.

Generously fill half of each round with the cooled filling. Fold the unfilled pastry side over the filling and pinch the edges together well, so that there are no gaps (it may help to use a little water to seal it together: dip your fingertip into a shallow bowl of water and trace around the edge). Twist and pinch the edges together or crimp with the tines of a fork, if desired.

Place the empanada on the prepared baking sheet and continue assembling until you run out of dough or filling.

Brush lightly with the olive oil and bake for 15 to 20 minutes. Remove from the oven.

Serve immediately with the Spiced Pear Chutney (page 131).

CHUTNEY

These chunky chutneys complement dishes with extra sweet, savory, spicy flavors. They're also a perfect way of preserving the harvest.

CHOOSE YOUR FAVORITE COMBINATION

BASE (2 pounds)

Apples

Chopped tomatillos + fresh cilantro (1 cup)

Cranberries

Mangoes

Pears

Peaches

Tomatoes

AROMATICS

Chili peppers (3)

Garlic (3)

Ginger (2-inch piece)

Shallots (1)

SPICES (1–2 teaspoons)

Curry powder

Dried oregano

Ground cardamom

Ground cumin

Ground turmeric

Peppercorns

Sweet paprika

SWEETNESS, OPTIONAL (1–2 tablespoons)

Brown rice syrup

Dates, pitted

Pure maple syrup

Raw cane sugar

ACIDITY (3 tablespoons)

Apple cider vinegar

Balsamic vinegar

Freshly squeezed lemon juice

Freshly squeezed lime juice

Freshly squeezed orange juice

Red wine vinegar

Rice vinegar

White wine vinegar

SALT (½ teaspoon)

SPICED PEAR CHUTNEY

MAKES 2 CUPS

1 pound pears, peeled and diced

2 dates, pitted and finely chopped

¼ cup rice vinegar

1 shallot, finely chopped

1 tablespoon freshly grated ginger

1 cinnamon stick

1 teaspoon ground turmeric

½ teaspoon salt

¼ teaspoon freshly ground black pepper

Pinch cayenne pepper

METHOD

Combine all of the ingredients in a medium stockpot over high heat and bring to a boil. Reduce the heat to low, cover, and simmer for 1 hour.

Raise the heat to high again and cook for 5 minutes, until the mixture thickens. Remove from the heat and set aside to cool completely. Use or store in the refrigerator in an airtight glass jar.

FALAFEL

When I lived in Hong Kong, a Lebanese restaurant around the corner from my home made fresh bread to order, which was perfect with creamy hummus and crispy falafel. This Asian twist on that dish celebrates that time in my life.

ASIAN EDAMAME FALAFEL

MAKES ABOUT 20 (1½-INCH) PATTIES

1 cup chickpea (gram) flour

1 cup filtered water

1 tablespoon olive oil

1 cup chopped fresh spinach

½ cup shelled and cooked edamame

¼ cup chopped fresh cilantro, leaves and stems

1 (½-inch) piece ginger, freshly grated

2 tablespoons chopped green onion

1 teaspoon five-spice powder

1 teaspoon tamari or soy sauce

Hummus (page 98), pita or naan bread, chopped kale, chopped green onion, pomegranate arils, chopped fresh cilantro, and tahini for serving

CHOOSE YOUR FAVORITE COMBINATION

BASE			
1 cup chickpea (gram) flour + 1 cup filtered water	Kale	Edamame	Dried parsley
	Spinach	Fresh herbs	Dried rosemary
or (2 cups, cooked)		Grilled red peppers	Dried sage
	AROMATICS (1–2 tablespoons)	Spinach	Dried tarragon
Cannellini beans	Fresh chives	Sunchokes (cooked)	Dried thyme
Chickpeas	Freshly grated ginger	Sweet potatoes (cooked)	Fennel seeds
Lima beans			Five-spice powder
Navy beans	Garlic	(¼ cup)	Freshly ground black pepper
	Green onion	Olives	
LEAFY GREENS (1 cup chopped)	Leeks	Sun-dried tomatoes	Ground cumin
	Onion		Salt
Bok choy	Shallots		Sweet paprika
Fresh basil		**SEASONINGS** (1–2 teaspoons)	Tamari or soy sauce
Fresh cilantro	**FLAVORS (½ cup)**	Curry powder	
Fresh mint	Artichoke hearts	Dried oregano	
Fresh parsley	Beets		

METHOD

Preheat the oven to 400°F.

In a blender or a food processor fitted with the "S" blade, combine the chickpea flour and blend until smooth.

In a large skillet over high heat, warm the olive oil. Add the spinach and sauté for 2 to 3 minutes until wilted. Remove from the heat and set aside to cool.

Place the cooled sautéed spinach in a paper towel and wring out all moisture. Add the spinach, edamame, cilantro, ginger, green onion, five-spice powder, and tamari or soy sauce to the blender or food processor and blend until well combined.

Turn out the falafel mixture onto a clean work surface and roll it, using the palms of your hands, into 20 balls that are about the size of walnuts. Squash them slightly—forming thick, compact patties—and place them on a baking sheet.

Bake for 20 to 30 minutes, or until crisp, flipping them over halfway through the baking time.

To serve, spread the hummus on the pita or naan bread and top it with the falafel, kale, green onion, pomegranate arils, and cilantro. Drizzle with the tahini and serve.

BETTER VEGGIE BURGERS

The only store-bought veggie burgers I've ever tried were promotional samples, and none of them impressed me. At the end of the day, even though they might be vegan, organic, gluten free, and/or non-GMO, they're still ultra-processed, and they still come in plastic packaging. Burgers are so easy to make, and you can be super flexible with the combination of ingredients. I keep some patties in the freezer to heat up when I need them. For the buns, I get them from bakeries that use paper bags for their baked goods, which I reuse for composting scraps in the freezer.

CHOOSE YOUR FAVORITE COMBINATION

LEGUMES (2 cups, cooked)

Adzuki

Black

Borlotti

Cannellini

Chickpeas

Navy

Pinto

Red kidney

VEGETABLES (1 cup)

Beets

Celery

Mushrooms

Spinach

ADDITIONS (½ cup)

Fresh basil

Fresh mint

Fresh parsley

Kale

Spinach

Walnuts

AROMATICS (2–3 tablespoons)

Fresh chives

Freshly grated ginger

Garlic

Green onion

Leeks

Onion

Shallots

GRAINS (1 cup, cooked)

Millet

Oats

Quinoa

Wild rice

or

Sweet potatoes

HERBS + SPICES (1–2 teaspoons)

Curry powder

Dried oregano

Dried parsley

Dried rosemary

Dried sage

Dried tarragon

Dried thyme

Freshly ground black pepper

Ground cumin

Ground fennel

Smoked paprika

ITALIAN-O BURGERS

MAKES 4 TO 6 SERVINGS

2 tablespoons olive oil, plus more
    for oiling the pan
1 leek, light green and white parts
    only, sliced
1 garlic clove, finely chopped
1 portobello mushroom, chopped
½ beet, chopped
¼ cup chopped kale
2 cups cooked cannellini beans

1 cup cooked quinoa
¼ cup finely chopped fresh parsley
1 teaspoon ground sage
1 teaspoon fennel seed
½ teaspoon salt
Lettuce, sliced tomatoes, sour-
    dough rolls, and Oil-Free
    Mayonnaise (page 62) for
    serving

METHOD

In a large skillet over high heat, warm the olive oil. Add the leek and sauté for 5 to 7 minutes until soft. Add the garlic, mushroom, and beet and cook for 5 more minutes, stirring occasionally. Add the kale and sauté until it wilts and no liquid is left in the pan. Remove from the heat and set aside to cool.

In a food processor fitted with the "S" blade, combine the cooked vegetables, beans, quinoa, parsley, sage, fennel seed, and salt and process until smooth.

Turn out the batter onto a clean work surface and divide it into four to six equal patties (or into balls for meatless balls) and place them on a baking sheet. Set aside to rest for 20 minutes.

To roast (making a sturdier burger), preheat the oven to 425°F and bake for 20 minutes, flipping once during the baking time. Remove from the oven.

To pan fry (making a moist burger), coat the skillet with olive oil over high heat. Add the patties and fry for 5 minutes on each side.

Serve with the lettuce, sliced tomatoes, sourdough rolls, and oil-free mayonnaise.

VEGGIE FRIES

I love these variations on fries—especially all the non-potato ones, as I can't eat potatoes without discomfort. Coating them gives them a really nice crunch, and baking them requires very little oil. These are best enjoyed immediately, to experience the warm comfort of the crispy and soft textures alike.

CHOOSE YOUR FAVORITE COMBINATION

VEGETABLES

Avocados (3)

Carrots (2 pounds)

Eggplant (1 pound)

Green beans
(1½ pounds)

Kohlrabi (4)

Parsnips (2 pounds)

Potatoes (4)

Sweet potatoes (3)

Taro (1 large)

Zucchini (4)

HERBS + SPICES
(1–2 teaspoons dried)

Curry powder

Dried oregano

Dried parsley

Dried rosemary

Dried sage

Dried tarragon

Dried thyme

Freshly ground
black pepper

Garlic powder

Ground cumin

Ground fennel

Smoked paprika

"EGG" MIXTURE

8 tablespoons
Aquafaba (page 27)

2 tablespoons
chia seeds + 6
tablespoons
filtered water

2 tablespoons
flax seed meal
+ 6 tablespoons
filtered water

CRISPY TOPPING
(½ cup)

Almond Flour
(page 83)

Chickpea (gram)
flour

Plant Milk Meal
(page 83)

(1 cup)

Panko

Vegan Parmesan
(page 191)

SEASONINGS
(1 teaspoon–3 tablespoons)

Chili powder

Dried basil

Dried parsley

Dried rosemary

Dried sage

Five-spice powder

Freshly ground
black pepper

Garlic powder

Ground cumin

Ground turmeric

Nutritional yeast

Salt

Smoked paprika

Sweet paprika

Za'atar

CONDIMENTS

Avocado Cream
(page 62)

Cashew Cream
(page 160)

Cashewgurt
(page 46)

Garlic Mayonnaise
(page 62)

Hoisin Sauce
(page 145)

Homemade
Harissa (page 126)

Nut Butter
(page 40)

Pesto (page 164)

Raw Marinara
Sauce (page 139)

Salsa (page 176)

BAKE TIMES

Avocados	12 to 15 minutes	Parsnips	25 to 35 minutes
Carrots	20 to 25 minutes	Potatoes	40 to 50 minutes
Eggplant	15 to 20 minutes	Sweet potatoes	15 to 25 minutes
Green beans	12 to 15 minutes	Taro	20 to 30 minutes
Kohlrabi	20 to 30 minutes	Zucchini	20 to 25 minutes

KOHLRABI FRIES

MAKES 4 SERVINGS

3 kohlrabi bulbs, peeled

6 tablespoons filtered water

2 tablespoons flax seed meal

1 cup chickpea (gram) flour

3 tablespoons nutritional yeast

2 teaspoons garlic powder

1 teaspoon salt

METHOD

Preheat the oven to 425°F. Slice the kohlrabi into 1-by-3-inch batons.

Combine the water and flax seed meal in a medium bowl and set aside to rest for 10 minutes.

Combine the chickpea flour with the spices and salt in a separate bowl and set aside. Dip the kohlrabi batons into the thickened flax seed meal, making sure each is evenly coated. Let any excess liquid drip off and then dredge in the seasoned flour (I've found that it's easier to coat them one or two at a time to get an even coating, as otherwise the flour gets lumpy).

Place the coated batons in a single layer on a baking sheet with about ½ inch of space between each. Bake for 20 to 30 minutes, turning them over after 10 minutes. Remove from the oven.

Serve immediately.

RAW MARINARA SAUCE

MAKES 3 CUPS

6 tomatoes (about 1½ pounds)

½ red bell pepper

10 sun-dried tomatoes

2 shallots

4 dates, pitted

2 garlic cloves

2 teaspoons apple cider vinegar

½ teaspoon salt

METHOD

In a blender or food processor fitted with the "S" blade, combine all of the ingredients and blend until smooth.

Serve or store in an airtight container in the refrigerator.

NOTE: You can enjoy this sauce with Zoodles (page 161) or as the base for any tomato sauce–based recipe, such as Chili (page 201) or Ratatian (page 185).

PLANT-BASED SUSHI

Sushi is always fun to make—and to eat, of course! Colorful vegan toppings and creative flavors and textures, along with a tasty, complementary sauce, will be enjoyed by even the most ardent seafood lover. It's best to make this recipe with fresh rice, rather than with leftover grains.

CHOOSE YOUR FAVORITE COMBINATION

RICE (4 cups, freshly cooked)

Forbidden

Purple sticky

Red

Short-grain, brown

Short-grain, white

DIPPING

Cashew Cream (page 160)

Chili Dipping Sauce (page 184)

TOPPINGS (1–2 cups, thinly sliced)

Avocados

Carrot Lox (page 65)

Crispy Tofu (page 163)

Cucumbers

Mangoes

Pekingbello (page 145)

Shiso leaves

Tomatuna (page 142)

SPRINKLES

Chili powder

Fresh chives

Freshly ground black pepper

Hemp seeds

HERBS

Freshly squeezed lime juice and zest

Green onion

Sesame seeds

DRESSING

Garlic Mayonnaise (page 62)

Scallion Ginger Sauce (page 184)

Hoisin Sauce (page 145)

Homemade Harissa (page 126)

Spicy Peanut Sauce (page 180)

Tamari or soy sauce

NIGIRI SUSHI BITES

MAKES ABOUT 32 PIECES

1 cup purple sticky rice, rinsed

1 cup white short-grain rice, rinsed

3½ cups filtered water

½ of an avocado, pitted and cut into strips

¼ of an English cucumber, peeled and cut into thin strips

8 slices Carrot Lox (page 65)

8 slices Pekingbello (page 145)

8 pieces Tomatuna (page 142)

1 red chili pepper, cut into strips

1 teaspoon fresh chives, finely chopped

¼ teaspoon freshly ground black pepper

(continued)

In a saucepan with a tight-fitting lid over high heat, combine the water and the purple and white rice and bring to a boil. Immediately reduce the heat to low, cover, and simmer for 20 to 30 minutes, or until all the water is absorbed. Remove from the heat, stir in the rice vinegar, cover with a dish towel, and set aside to cool slightly (it should still be warm, but not too hot to handle).

With wet hands, form 2 tablespoons of warm rice into bite-size logs. Place strips of the avocado, cucumber, carrot lox, pekingbello, tomatuna, and/or red chili pepper on top of the logs and sprinkle with the chives and black pepper.

Slice and serve at room temperature with the dipping sauce of your choice.

NEGI TOMATUNA

4 small tomatoes, ripe but not too soft

6 tablespoons chopped fresh chives

¼ cup tamari or soy sauce

2 teaspoons sesame oil

1 teaspoon dulse flakes

½ teaspoon freshly grated ginger

¼ teaspoon pure maple syrup

METHOD

Fill a large bowl with water and ice.

Place a small saucepan ¾ of the way full of water over high heat and bring to a boil.

Using a sharp knife, make an "X" incision at the base of each tomato. Place the tomatoes into the boiling water for 30 seconds to 1 minute, or until the skins start to peel off. Immediately remove the tomatoes and place them in the ice bath to stop the cooking process. Remove from the heat.

Peel and discard the tomatoes' skins and slice them into large chunks. Remove the seeds and save them for Root-to-Leaf Stock (page 215) or a savory Super Smoothie (page 86).

In a large bowl, combine the tomatoes with the remaining ingredients and refrigerate for 30 minutes to overnight, turning occasionally so the mixture marinates evenly.

Serve or store refrigerated in an airtight jar.

LOADED SWEET POTATOES

Sweet potatoes are a good low-glycemic carbohydrate. They're high in fiber, potassium, and nutritional value, and we like them steamed as a handy, high-energy snack. You can load them with a variety of toppings for a substantial meal in place of starchy grains or potatoes. I've used them here in place of a Chinese steamed bun. In my opinion, this is one of the most delicious flavor combinations there is—hoisin sauce, cucumber, green onion, and a "meaty" roasted portobello mushroom.

SWEET POTATOES
(1 per person)

FILLING

Chili (page 201)

Dumpling filling
(page 181)

Empanada filling
(page 127)

Jerk Cauliflower
(page 212)

Ratatian (page 185)

Stew (page 203)

Tofu Scramble
(page 66)

TOPPINGS

Arugula

Asparagus

Avocados

Carrots

Cucumbers

Leafy greens

Pickles (page 151)

Quinoa

Radishes

Sun-dried
tomatoes

Tomatoes

CONDIMENTS

Cashew Cream
(page 160)

Cashewgurt
(page 46)

Hoisin Sauce
(page 145)

Homemade
Harissa (page 126)

Hummus (page 98)

Kimchi (page 153)

Nut Butter
(page 40)

Oil-Free
Mayonnaise
(page 62)

Pesto (page 164)

Roasted Eggplant
Dip (page 170)

Salsa (page 176)

Spicy Peanut
Sauce (page 180)

SPRINKLES

Chili peppers

Fresh chives

Fresh herbs

Green onions

Microgreens

Olives

FOR THE SWEET POTATOES

1 sweet potato

METHOD

WHOLE ROASTED: Preheat the oven to 425°F. Pierce the sweet potato all over with a fork and place it on a baking sheet. Roast for about 40 minutes, or until soft (if it's really big, cut it in half lengthwise and roast it cut-side down on a piece of parchment paper). This can be eaten right away, or set aside to cool completely before storing in the refrigerator. When it's time to eat, simply reheat it, cut it in half, load it up, and enjoy.

STEAMED: Place a halved sweet potato in a steamer basket inside a large pot over medium-high heat containing 1 inch of boiling water. Cover and steam for 20 to 25 minutes, depending on how large the halves are, or until they pierce easily with a fork. Remove from the heat. This can be eaten right away, or set aside to cool completely before storing in the refrigerator. When it's time to eat, simply reheat it, load it up, and enjoy.

PEKINGBELLO SANDWICH

MAKES 2 SERVINGS

2 whole portobello mushrooms

2 small sweet potatoes

2 tablespoons Hoisin Sauce
(recipe follows)

1 teaspoon sesame oil

¼ teaspoon cayenne pepper

1 (4-inch) segment cucumber,
julienned

6 radicchio leaves

1 green onion, julienned

1 red chili pepper, sliced

METHOD

Using a clean dish towel, brush any dirt off the mushrooms. Cut the sweet potatoes in half lengthwise.

Preheat the oven to 425°F. Line a baking sheet with parchment paper.

In a small bowl, stir together the hoisin sauce, sesame oil, and cayenne pepper. Slather the mixture on the mushrooms, top and bottom. Place the coated mushrooms on the prepared baking sheet, cap-side up. Place the sweet potatoes, cut-side down, next to them.

Roast the mushrooms and the sweet potatoes for 20 minutes, flipping them over after 10 minutes. Remove from the oven. Set aside to cool slightly.

Slice the mushrooms and load them on top of the sweet potatoes. Top with the cucumber, radicchio, green onion, and chili pepper and serve.

HOISIN SAUCE

MAKES ABOUT ½ CUP

8 dried prunes, soaked and
drained

¼ cup coconut sugar

2 tablespoons filtered water

2 tablespoons tamari or soy sauce

2 teaspoons rice vinegar

1 teaspoon toasted sesame oil

½ teaspoon five-spice powder

¼ teaspoon garlic powder

METHOD

In a blender, combine all of the ingredients and blend until smooth. Transfer to an airtight glass jar and store in the refrigerator.

FRIED RICE

Fried rice is the ultimate go-to for leftovers. It's just as easy to make a big batch of rice or other grains as it is a small one, and once you have those leftovers, you can be creative with them. Combine little bits of anything in your fridge, add a few more fresh or frozen ingredients, and you have an instant one-dish meal. The fried rice served in restaurants is usually 90 percent grains and 10 percent vegetables or meat, but when you make it at home, use a 50:50 ratio of grains to everything else. Load it with plenty of nutritious ingredients to make it a more balanced meal for any time of day—even breakfast. We have this in the morning once in a while. Sometimes, I like adding finely chopped cauliflower to the rice for a sneaky nutritious boost. It passed the test when I got the thumbs up from two super picky eaters! (Thank goodness, because I had chopped it all by hand that time!)

CHOOSE YOUR FAVORITE COMBINATION

GRAINS (2-3 cups, cooked)

Cauliflower, riced

Millet

Quinoa

Rice (basmati, brown, black, jasmine, red, or wild)

AROMATICS (1-3 tablespoons)

Fresh chives

Freshly grated ginger

Garlic

Green onion

Leeks

Onion

Shallots

OIL (2 tablespoons)

Coconut

Olive

Sesame, light

Sunflower seed

VEGETABLES (1 cup)

Asparagus

Broccoli

Carrot

Corn

Edamame

Green beans

Kimchi (page 153)

Peas

Snow peas

Zucchini

LEAFY GREENS, FINELY CHOPPED (1-2 cups)

Bok choy

Cabbage

Chard

Fresh herbs

Kale

Spinach

SEASONING (to taste)

Freshly ground black pepper

Nutritional yeast

Salt

Soy sauce

Tamari or soy sauce

GARDEN FRIED RICE

MAKES 2 SERVINGS

2 tablespoons olive oil

1 cup riced cauliflower

1 shallot, finely chopped

1 cup garden peas

1 cup chopped Swiss chard

2 cups cooked brown rice

3 tablespoons nutritional yeast

¼ cup chopped fresh mint

Freshly grated zest and freshly
   squeezed juice of ½ lemon

½ teaspoon salt or to taste

¼ teaspoon freshly ground black
   pepper or to taste

METHOD

In a frying pan large enough to hold all of the ingredients over high heat, warm the olive oil. Sauté the cauliflower and shallot for 3 minutes, or until they have softened. Add the garden peas and chard, tossing to combine, and cook for 5 more minutes. Finally, add the rice and nutritional yeast and cook for 1 more minute. Remove from the heat.

Transfer to a serving bowl. Add the mint, lemon juice, and zest and season with the salt and pepper. Toss well and serve.

RAINBOWLS

Whether you call them Rainbowls, Dragon Bowls, Buddha Bowls, or Macro Bowls, the combinations are endless—especially with the change of seasons. Incorporating a variety of textures and flavors, as well as proteins and fermented foods, ensures a balanced meal. Most of my meals are structured this way, as I grab little bits of leftovers to create a different meal every time. Select four or five raw and/or cooked vegetables for variety.

SPRING: Purple rice, black beans, pickled carrot ribbons, grilled garlic scapes (stalks), snow peas, garden peas, strawberries, watermelon, purple radishes, pea microgreens, and chives.

SUMMER: Beet Hummus (page 98), quinoa, pan-roasted baby artichokes, cherry tomatoes, baby zucchini, green beans, blueberries, and cucumber Zoodles (page 161).

AUTUMN: Purple rice, black beans, steamed butternut squash, Pickled Peppers (page 151), corn, tomatoes, red cabbage, and parsley.

WINTER: Quinoa, French lentils, roasted sweet potatoes, honeynut squash, steamed romanesco, Brussels sprouts, sautéed mushrooms, and chioggia beet slices.

CHOOSE YOUR FAVORITE COMBINATION

BASE (1 cup)

Cauliflower rice
Millet
Quinoa
Rice
Zoodles (page 161)

PROTEIN (½ cup)

Edamame
Hummus (page 98)
Legumes (page 26)
Lentils
Tofu

SEAWEED

Hijiki
Nori
Wakame

**VEGETABLES
(½ cup × 2, raw)**

Arugula
Asparagus
Avocados
Beets
Broccoli
Brussels sprouts
Carrots
Cauliflower
Celery
Cucumber
Fennel
Green beans
Kale
Kohlrabi
Lettuce
Peppers
Radishes

Snap peas
Sprouts (page 24)
Tomatoes
Zucchini

**VEGETABLES
(½ cup × 2, cooked)**

Artichokes
Asparagus
Bok choy
Broccoli
Brussels sprouts
Butternut squash
Cauliflower
Corn
Eggplant
Fennel
Green beans
Mushrooms
Okra

Parsnips
Peppers
Potatoes
Pumpkin
Romanesco
Sweet potatoes
Turnips
Zucchini

**OTHER
FERMENTED
(3–4 tablespoons)**

Kimchi (page 153)
Pickles (page 151)
Sauerkraut

**HEALTHY FAT
(1 tablespoon)**

Any homemade
Dressing (page 116)

REFRIGERATOR PICKLES

Pickling foods at home is a simple, fun, and creative way to preserve the harvest. I always get a lot of chili peppers from my community-supported agriculture (CSA) farm share, so I pickle a portion of these. The pickling brine can also be used as a marinade, as an ingredient in a flavorful salad dressing, or as a way to add umami flavors to recipes like Mock "Tuna" (page 61). I purchase my spices in bulk in my own jars at the food co-op.

CHOOSE YOUR FAVORITE COMBINATION

VEGETABLES (2 cups chopped)

Asparagus	Cucumbers
Beets	Garlic
Beets + chard stems	Green beans
	Jicama
Bell peppers	Leeks
Brussels sprouts	Onions
Cabbage	Radishes
Carrots	Rhubarb
Cauliflower	Shallots
Celery	Zucchini
Chilies	

OR FRUIT

Berries	Pineapple
Cherries	Plums
Grapes	Rhubarb
Peaches	Quinces

LIQUID (1 cup)

Filtered water

+

1 teaspoon salt

SEASONINGS (2 tablespoons)

Aleppo pepper

Bay leaves

Caraway seeds

Cloves

Coriander seeds

Cumin seeds

Dill

Dried lavender

Dried rosemary

Dried thyme

Freshly grated ginger

Garlic

Ground cinnamon

Homemade Harissa (page 126)

Lemon zest

Mustard seeds

Peppercorns

Star anise

VINEGAR (1 cup)

Apple cider

Red wine

Rice

White

SWEETENER, OPTIONAL (1 tablespoon)

Coconut sugar

Maple sugar

Raw cane sugar

PICKLED CAULIFLOWER

2 cups chopped cauliflower

1 garlic clove

1 tablespoon Aleppo pepper

1 cup rice vinegar

1 cup filtered water

1 teaspoon salt

PICKLED HOLY MOLE PEPPERS

2 cups sliced holy mole peppers

1 tablespoon mustard seeds

1 tablespoon cumin seeds

1 cup white vinegar

1 cup filtered water

1 teaspoon salt

PICKLED RHUBARB

2 cups sliced rhubarb

1 tablespoon mustard seeds

2 star anise

1 cup apple cider vinegar

1 cup filtered water

1 tablespoon raw cane sugar

1 teaspoon salt

METHOD

Place the cleaned, cut vegetables and seasonings in a canning jar that has been rinsed with boiling hot water.

In a small saucepan over high heat, combine the vinegar, water, sugar (if using), and salt and bring to a boil. Reduce the heat to low and simmer for 5 minutes, stirring until the sugar (if using) and salt dissolves. Remove from the heat.

Pour the hot vinegar mixture into the veggie-filled jar, pushing down the contents to ensure they stay submerged. Fill until only ½ inch of air space remains. Seal the jar and leave it on the countertop until it's cool to the touch, and then refrigerate.

NOTE: Like Kimchi (page 153), these pickled vegetables will last for a few months in your refrigerator. If it smells rotten or if mold has formed, it should be composted.

KIMCHI

Good bacteria, or probiotics, keep your body in balance. Processed foods, medicines, and chemicals, including toxins from plastics, wreak havoc on our natural supply of good bacteria in our guts. Eating just 2 to 4 tablespoons of fermented foods a day will help improve digestion, strengthen immunity, prevent diseases, and fight inflammation. Start each day with a small amount of fermented food to get your body accustomed to the good bugs, and then gradually increase to what feels best for you. When you make this recipe, you can always enjoy some of the kimchi right away, but the flavors and good enzymes don't really kick in until after it has aged for a few days. I always keep a jar of kimchi in the fridge available to serve up at any meal—or just to jazz up a bowl of plain rice.

CHOOSE YOUR FAVORITE COMBINATION

LEAFY VEGETABLES
(2 pounds), cut or torn
into 3-inch pieces

Brussels sprouts, halved

Cabbage

Kale

Napa cabbage

Red cabbage

Savoy cabbage

BRINE

4 cups filtered water

+

¼ cup kosher salt

OTHER VEGETABLES,
sliced into rounds and
quartered (2 cups)

Cucumbers

Daikons

Radishes

ADDITIONS (½ cup)

Carrots, julienned

Garlic scapes (stalks)

Green onions

KIMCHI PASTE

1 head garlic

+

1 (1-inch) piece ginger,
freshly grated

+

⅓ cup gochugaru (Korean
red pepper flakes) or
Aleppo pepper flakes

+

⅓ cup rice vinegar

+

½ pear, peeled

+

2 tablespoons sesame
seeds

BRUSSELS SPROUTS KIMCHI

1 pound Brussels sprouts, sliced
    in half lengthwise

1 daikon, peeled and sliced into
    rounds

¼ cup kosher salt

4 cups filtered water

½ pear, peeled

1 head garlic

⅓ cup Aleppo pepper

⅓ cup rice vinegar

1 (1-inch) piece ginger, freshly
    grated

2 tablespoons sesame seeds

1 carrot, cut into matchsticks

METHOD

Combine the Brussels sprouts and daikon in a large mixing bowl. Sprinkle with the salt and massage the salt into the vegetables. Add the water, place a heavy plate on top to keep the vegetables submerged, and set aside for 30 minutes.

In a small food processor fitted with the "S" blade or an immersion blender, combine the pear, garlic, Aleppo pepper, rice vinegar, ginger, and sesame seeds and process until a thick paste forms. You can also make this paste with a large mortar and pestle.

Drain the vegetables, reserving the brine, and transfer them to a bowl. Set aside.

Add the spice paste and the carrot to the bowl containing the salted vegetables and mix until well combined.

Transfer the kimchi into airtight glass canning jars. Tightly pack it into the jar and add some of the reserved brine, making sure to leave 1 inch of airspace from the top. Seal and leave at room temperature to ferment for 2 to 3 days and nights (or in colder weather, for 5 nights). Open the jar slightly every other day to release any trapped air.

After the fermentation process is complete, store in the refrigerator.

NOTE: Kimchi lasts for quite a few months in the refrigerator. Only discard it if mold forms throughout the jar or if it smells rotten.

STIR-FRY

I love the ease and flexibility of a stir-fry. Most Chinese restaurants have on hand all the mix-and-match options necessary to have an impressively large menu of stir-fry delights, but a stir-fry isn't necessarily limited to Asian flavors. It's a quick way to prepare meals with just about anything on hand.

CHOOSE YOUR FAVORITE COMBINATION

OIL (2 tablespoons)

Coconut

Olive

Sesame (light)

Sunflower seed

AROMATICS (2–3 tablespoons)

Fresh chives

Ginger

Garlic

Green onion

Leeks

Onion

Shallots

SEASONING (to taste)

Salt

Tamari or soy sauce

VEGETABLES (4 cups, any combination)

Asparagus

Beans

Beets

Broccoli

Cabbage

Carrots

Celery

Edamame

Fennel

Leafy greens

Mushrooms

Peppers

Snap peas

Snow peas

Zucchini

HERBS & SPICES (1–2 teaspoons)

Curry powder

Dried oregano

Dried parsley

Dried rosemary

Dried sage

Dried tarragon

Dried thyme

Five-spice

Freshly ground black pepper

Ground cumin

Ground fennel

Smoked paprika

White pepper

SPRINKLES (2–3 tablespoons)

Chili flakes

Dukkah

Fresh chives

Fresh herbs

Freshly ground black pepper

Freshly squeezed citrus juice and zest

Green onions

Hemp seeds

Microgreens

Sesame seeds

Sprouts (page 24)

ROSEMARY AND ROOT VEGETABLE STIR-FRY

MAKES 4 SERVINGS

3 carrots

3 sunchokes

2 small chioggia beets

1 zucchini

2 tablespoons olive oil

2 garlic cloves, minced

1 teaspoon chopped fresh sage

3 sprigs fresh rosemary

1 teaspoon freshly squeezed lemon juice

Salt to taste

Freshly ground black pepper to taste

METHOD

Scrub the carrots, beets, and zucchini, peel the sunchokes, and slice them into ¼-inch rounds.

In a large skillet over high heat, warm the olive oil. Add the garlic and sauté for 1 to 2 minutes, or until fragrant.

Add the carrots, sunchokes, beets, sage, and rosemary to the skillet and cook for 8 more minutes, or until the carrots have softened.

Add the zucchini slices to the skillet and cook for 3 more minutes, or until they are translucent. Remove from the heat.

Transfer the stir-fry to a serving dish and finish it off with the lemon juice. Season with the salt and black pepper, toss well, and serve.

PASTA

I have always loved creamy pastas more than tomato-based ones, but I can't tolerate the dairy. Did you know that 75 percent of the world's population is lactose intolerant? Cashew Cream (page 160) is the perfect substitute, without all the heaviness. We also love to add a little Mushroom Bacon (page 160). I always have to make a large batch of the bacon, because it disappears so quickly—even before I can get it on the plate!

NOODLES	SAUCE	TOPPINGS
16 ounces dried spaghetti noodles	Cashew Cream (page 160)	Arugula
	Creamy Soup (page 118)	Cashew Cheese (page 101)
or	Curry (page 194)	
VEGETABLE NOODLES (2 cups per person)	Oil-Free Mayonnaise (page 62)	Falafel (page 132)
	Pesto (page 164)	Mushroom Bacon (page 160)
Beet		Olive oil
Carrot	Raw Marinara Sauce (page 139)	Vegetables (cooked and raw)
Celery root	Dressing (page 116)	
Daikon	Spicy Peanut Sauce (page 180)	
Jicama		
Kohlrabi		
Zucchini		

CREAMY SPAGHETTI CARBONARA

MAKES 4 SERVINGS

16 ounces brown rice spaghetti

1 tablespoon salt

Cashew Cream (recipe follows)

Mushroom Bacon (recipe follows)

2 bunches broccolini, chopped and blanched (see note)

METHOD

Bring a large stockpot filled with water and the salt over high heat. Bring to a boil. Add the spaghetti and cook for about 10 minutes, or until al dente. Remove from the heat, rinse with cold water, and drain.

Return the spaghetti to the pot and mix well with the cashew cream and mushroom bacon. Top with the broccolini, toss, and serve.

NOTE: I like to blanch my vegetables, like this broccolini or a few handfuls of peas, with any pasta dish by throwing them in the pot during the last minute of cooking the pasta. It saves time—and washing up! If you are doing this in advance, make sure to rinse the drained pasta and vegetables with cold water to prevent the vegetables from overcooking. Otherwise, serve it right away.

CASHEW CREAM

1 cup organic raw cashews, soaked for 3 hours or overnight, drained, and rinsed

½ cup filtered water

3 tablespoons nutritional yeast

2 tablespoons freshly squeezed lemon juice

1 garlic clove

½ teaspoon apple cider vinegar

½ teaspoon salt

METHOD

In a blender or food processor fitted with the "S blade, combine all of the ingredients and blend until smooth.

Use immediately or store in an airtight jar in the refrigerator.

NOTE: For a sweet variation on this recipe for topping breakfast and dessert items, substitute 1 to 2 tablespoons of maple syrup for the nutritional yeast, lemon juice, garlic, vinegar, and salt.

MUSHROOM BACON

20 fresh shiitake mushrooms

3 tablespoons olive oil

2 tablespoons pure maple syrup

2 tablespoons low-sodium tamari or soy sauce

1 teaspoon smoked paprika

METHOD

Using a clean dish towel, brush any dirt off the mushrooms. Remove the stems and reserve them for use in the Root-to-Leaf Stock (page 215). Using a sharp knife, slice the mushrooms into ⅛-inch-thick slices.

Preheat the oven to 400°F. Line two baking sheets with parchment paper.

In a medium bowl, stir together the olive oil, maple syrup, tamari or soy sauce, and smoked paprika until well combined. Toss the mushroom slices into the bowl until evenly coated. Place them on the prepared baking sheet in a single layer.

Bake for 15 to 17 minutes, or until the mushrooms are fully dried, turning them over once or twice during the baking time. The slices in the center of the tray might take longer than those closer to the edges; make sure that you check them frequently during the last few minutes of the baking time so they don't burn and get bitter. Remove from the oven.

Serve or store in the refrigerator.

OODLES OF ZOODLES

I'm so grateful to the person who made making noodles out of vegetables so popular! Whether you use a vegetable peeler, mandolin, spiralizer, or a knife to hand cut the veggies into strips, they're a perfect vehicle for any sauce and provide a much more substantial meal with no empty carbs. Add them to a Rainbowl (page 148) or as a side for any meal like Dumplings (page 181). You can eat a simple bowl of Zoodles with Pesto (page 164) or Raw Marinara Sauce (page 139) and feel great and well nourished. Or if you're like me and can't resist a comforting bowl of noodle soup, then these are perfect for it . . . without all the usual MSG and additives and of course, the plastic packaging. If you seek a plastic-free way to purchase traditional noodles, visit a restaurant that makes them and bring along your own container for takeout. You can also find dried noodles and pasta in the bulk-food section of some stores—be sure to bring your own bag or container.

CHOOSE YOUR FAVORITE COMBINATION

VEGETABLE NOODLES
(2 cups per person)

Beets

Carrots

Celery root

Daikon

Kohlrabi

Zucchini

RAW ONLY

Cucumber

COOKED ONLY

Butternut squash

Parsnips

Sweet potatoes

SAUCY (½ cup per person)

Cashew Cream (page 160)

Creamy Soup (page 118)

Curry (page 194)

Hummus (page 98)

Oil-Free Mayonnaise
(page 62)

Pesto (page 164)

Raw Marinara Sauce
(page 139)

Dressing (page 116)

Spicy Peanut Sauce
(page 180)

TOPPINGS

Arugula

Chili flakes or fresh chilies

Meatless Balls (page 136)

Olive oil

Mushroom Bacon
(page 160)

Vegan Parmesan
(page 191)

Vegetables (cooked and raw)

SOUPY (2 cups per person)

Curry (page 194)

Miso soup

Root-to-Leaf Stock
(page 215)

TOPPINGS

Chili flakes (or fresh)

Crispy Tofu (page 163)

Green onions

Kimchi (page 153)

Mushrooms

Pickles (page 151)

Sesame seeds

Vegetables (cooked)

SWEET POTATO ZOODLE SOUP

MAKES 2 SERVINGS

1 large sweet potato (any color)

4 cups filtered water

3 tablespoons miso paste

2 carrots, sliced

6 shiitake mushrooms

1 small head broccoli, cut into
   bite-size pieces

½ cup fresh edamame, shelled

Crispy Tofu (recipe follows) for
   topping

Sauerkraut for topping

METHOD

Scrub the sweet potato. Peel and spiralize it into thick noodles.

In a medium stockpot over high heat, bring the water to a boil.

Spoon the miso paste into a small heatproof bowl and add ¼ cup of the boiling water to dilute the paste. Stir the mixture and then pour it back into the pot.

Add the carrots and mushrooms to the pot, reduce the heat to medium, and cook for 5 minutes. Add the sweet potato zoodles, broccoli, and edamame, return to a boil, and cook for 3 more minutes, or until the zoodles are soft and the broccoli still retains a slight crunch. (Don't let them boil for too long, or else the zoodles will fall apart.) Remove from the heat.

Evenly divide the vegetables and soup into two serving bowls. Top each with the crispy tofu and a few spoonfuls of the sauerkraut and serve.

CRISPY TOFU

1 pound firm tofu

3 tablespoons brown rice flour

½ teaspoon salt

2 tablespoons olive oil

1 shallot, finely chopped

2 garlic cloves, minced

1 (½-inch) piece ginger, grated

½ teaspoon crushed Sichuan
    peppercorns

METHOD

Using a clean dish towel folded in half, wrap the tofu so both the top and bottom are covered with a few layers of the towel. Place it on a cutting board and place a heavy skillet on top to press all of the liquid out of the tofu; set aside for 15 to 20 minutes.

Slice the tofu into 1-inch cubes.

Place the flour and salt in a bowl and dredge the cubes in the mixture until lightly coated.

In a large skillet over medium-high heat, warm the olive oil. Add the tofu cubes and fry for 2 minutes on each side, or until they are crisped and nicely golden. When all of the sides are crisped, add the shallot, garlic, ginger, and peppercorns and sauté for 3 to 5 more minutes, tossing until well combined. Remove from the heat.

Serve immediately.

PESTO

Pesto is a good complement when added to toasts, hummus, grains, soups, salad dressings, and marinades. It can also be frozen in small batches for use any time. You can always prepare this using a mortar and pestle, but if you're pressed for time, use a food processor or blender. Pesto is a great way to use up herbs and greens and keep them from spoiling.

CHOOSE YOUR FAVORITE COMBINATION

GREENS (3–4 cups chopped)

Carrot greens
Fresh basil
Fresh cilantro
Fresh dill
Fresh mint
Fresh parsley
Kale
Microgreens
Spinach

AROMATICS (1–3 pieces)

Garlic cloves
Garlic scapes (stalks)

TEXTURE (¼ cup)

Almonds
Cashews
Pepitas (pumpkin seeds)
Pine nuts
Pistachios (shelled)
Sunflower seeds
Walnuts

SEASONING

½ teaspoon salt

+

2–3 tablespoons nutritional yeast

ACIDITY (2 teaspoons)

Apple cider vinegar
Freshly squeezed lemon juice
Freshly squeezed lime juice
Rice vinegar
Wine vinegar

OIL (¼–½ cup, to desired consistency)

Avocado
Nut
Olive

KALE PESTO

MAKES 4 SERVINGS

4 cups kale
¼ cup olive oil, plus more as needed
¼ cup sunflower seeds

3 tablespoons nutritional yeast
1 garlic clove
2 teaspoons apple cider vinegar
¼ teaspoon salt

METHOD

Remove the leaves from the stems of the kale, saving the stems for a batch of Root-to-Leaf Stock (page 215) or for a Super Smoothie (page 86).

Place the leaves, ¼ cup olive oil, sunflower seeds, nutritional yeast, garlic, vinegar, and salt in a food processor fitted with the "S" blade and process into a smooth paste. Add as much as 1 to 2 teaspoons more olive oil if needed to reach the desired consistency.

Serve or store refrigerator in an airtight container.

PIZZA

Following inspirational foodie accounts on Instagram opened my eyes to the vast array of beautiful, veggie-loaded pizzas out there, many of which include wholesome crusts made from vegetables and plant protein. They're a far cry from the traditional cheese, tomato sauce, and white flour crust standard that looms large at nearly every kids' party or event. This is a simple one that celebrates the freshness of end-of-summer heirloom tomatoes and the delights of pesto.

CHOOSE YOUR FAVORITE COMBINATION

CRUST

Flatbreads (page 168)

Flour Tortillas (page 174)

SPREAD

Hummus (page 98)

Mushroom Tapenade (page 109)

Nut Cheese (page 101)

Pesto (page 164)

Raw Marinara Sauce (page 139)

Roasted Eggplant Dip (page 170)

Salsa (page 176)

Sweet potatoes (cooked and mashed)

TOPPINGS

Arugula

Avocados

Beets

Bell peppers

Broccoli

Corn

Figs

Fresh herbs

Green onions

Jalapeño peppers

Legumes (cooked)

Lettuce

Mushrooms

Nuts

Red onion

Spinach

Tomatoes

Zucchini

SPRINKLES

Chili flakes

Dukkah

Fresh chives

Fresh herbs

Freshly ground black pepper

Freshly squeezed citrus juice and zest

Green onion

Hemp seeds

Microgreens

Nutritional yeast

Sesame seeds

Sprouts (page 24)

Vegan Parmesan (page 191)

HEIRLOOM TOMATO PIZZA

1 recipe Cauliflower Chickpea Flatbread (page 168)

2 cups Kale Pesto (page 164)

4–5 heirloom tomatoes in a variety of colors, sliced

Fresh basil for topping

Salt to taste

Freshly ground black pepper to taste

METHOD

Preheat the oven to 400°F. Line a baking sheet with parchment paper.

Prepare the cauliflower chickpea flatbread (page 168).

Bake for 20 minutes, flipping the crust over after 10 minutes to ensure even cooking. Remove from the oven and set aside to cool for 5 minutes.

Spread the kale pesto on the baked crust and arrange the tomatoes over it in a single layer. Arrange the basil on top and season with salt and black pepper. Serve.

FLATBREADS AND PIZZA CRUSTS

I love that these crusts add flavor, nutrients, and a bit of color to an otherwise very plain pizza base. You can also slice them into strips and enjoy them with your favorite dip, such as Roasted Eggplant Dip (page 170).

CHOOSE YOUR FAVORITE COMBINATION

VEGETABLES (6 ounces)	BASE	FLOUR (¾ cup to 1 cup)
Beet	¼ cup ground flax seeds	Buckwheat
Butternut squash	+	Chickpea (gram)
Carrot	1 teaspoon garlic powder	Oat
Cauliflower	+	Spelt
Celery root	½ teaspoon salt	Whole wheat
Parsnip	+	
Potato	½ cup filtered water	
Sweet potato		

BUTTERNUT SPELT FLATBREAD

6 ounces cooked butternut
squash (about 2 cups)

1 cup spelt flour

¼ cup ground flax seeds

1 teaspoon garlic powder

½ teaspoon salt

½ cup filtered water

CAULIFLOWER CHICKPEA FLATBREAD

6 ounces raw cauliflower florets
(about 2 cups)

1 cup chickpea (gram) flour

¼ cup ground flax seeds

1 teaspoon garlic powder

½ teaspoon salt

½ cup filtered water

BEETROOT BUCKWHEAT FLATBREAD

2 small beets, roasted
(about 6 ounces)

½ cup whole wheat flour

¼ cup buckwheat flour

¼ cup ground flax seeds

1 teaspoon garlic powder

½ teaspoon salt

½ cup filtered water, plus more
as needed

METHOD

To make the "dough": Combine all of the ingredients in a food processor fitted with the "S" blade and process into a thick, pourable paste; add more water if needed. Set aside to rest for 20 to 30 minutes.

To bake: Preheat the oven to 400°F and line a baking sheet with parchment paper.

Spread the batter on the prepared baking sheet and bake for 20 minutes, flipping it over after 10 minutes. Remove from the oven.

ROASTED EGGPLANT DIP (BABAGANOUSH)

1 large eggplant

5 garlic cloves, tossed in
    1 teaspoon of olive oil, to coat

3 tablespoons freshly squeezed
    lemon juice

2 tablespoons tahini

1 teaspoon ground cumin

¼ teaspoon cayenne pepper

¼ teaspoon salt

3 tablespoons olive oil, plus more
    as needed

Fresh parsley leaves for garnish

METHOD

Preheat the oven to 425°F.

Using the tines of a fork, pierce the eggplant all over at least a dozen times and place it on a baking sheet; place the garlic cloves next to it. Roast for 35 to 45 minutes, turning several times during the roasting time to ensure even cooking. Remove from the oven and set aside to cool.

Halve the eggplant lengthwise and scoop out the soft insides. Place them in a large bowl. Pop the garlic cloves out of their skins and add the cloves to the bowl, along with the lemon juice, tahini, cumin, cayenne pepper, salt, and olive oil. Using a fork or wooden spatula, smash the mixture together—you don't need any electrical appliances for this. Cover and chill in the refrigerator.

Just before serving, drizzle the mixture with a little more olive oil and garnish with the parsley.

TACOS

Tacos every day, I say! This is yet another perfect way to revitalize leftovers—just add a few fresh ingredients, as well as some staple condiments you might have on hand. I try to make a few batches of Flour Tortillas (page 174) on the weekend so I always have a stack in the freezer at the ready.

CHOOSE YOUR FAVORITE COMBINATION

TORTILLAS
(8; page 174)

FILLING (2–3 cups)

Cauliflower
Legumes (cooked)
Mushrooms
Sweet potatoes
Tofu

+

(2 tablespoons)

Coconut butter
Coconut oil
Olive oil

SPICES (2–3 teaspoons)

Cayenne pepper
Dried basil
Dried oregano
Dried parsley
Dried rosemary

Dried sage
Dried thyme
Five-spice powder
Garam masala
Ground cardamom
Ground cumin
Ground ginger
Ground turmeric
Smoked paprika
Sweet paprika

TOPPINGS (2 cups, mixed)

Artichoke hearts
Arugula
Avocados
Bell peppers
Broccoli
Cabbage
Carrots
Corn
Fresh cilantro

Jalapeño peppers
Lettuce
Quinoa
Red onion
Spinach
Tomatoes
Walnuts
Zucchini

SPRINKLES (2–3 tablespoons)

Chili flakes
Dukkah
Fresh chives
Fresh herbs
Freshly grated citrus zest
Freshly ground black pepper
Freshly squeezed citrus juice
Green onion

Hemp seeds
Microgreens
Sesame seeds
Sprouts (page 24)

CONDIMENTS (to taste)

Cashew Cream (page 160)
Chutney (page 131)
Hoisin Sauce (page 145)
Homemade Harissa (page 126)
Kimchi (page 153)
Oil-Free Mayonnaise (page 62)
Pesto (page 164)
Pickles (page 151)

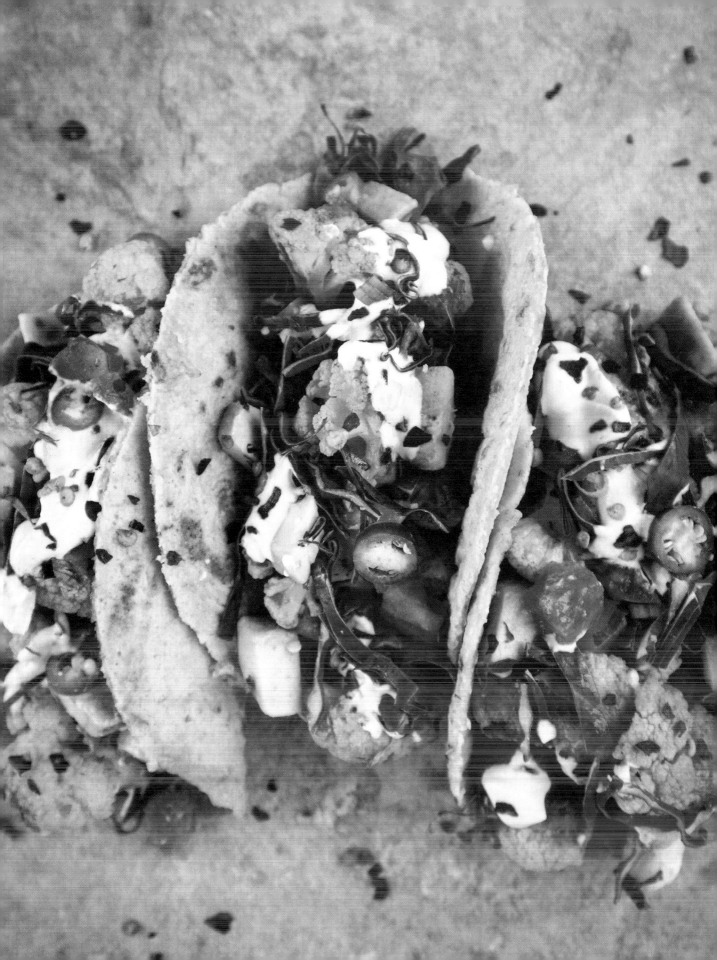

COCONUT LIME CAULIFLOWER TACOS

MAKES 8

2 tablespoons coconut butter

½ onion, finely chopped

1 garlic clove, minced

1 small head cauliflower, cut into bite-size florets

1 teaspoon ground cumin

1 teaspoon ground turmeric

½ teaspoon smoked paprika

½ teaspoon cayenne pepper

2 tablespoons filtered water (optional)

½ teaspoon salt

¼ teaspoon freshly ground black pepper

¼ cup chopped fresh cilantro

Freshly grated zest and freshly squeezed juice of 1 lime

8 Flour Tortillas (page 174)

Sliced avocado, red cabbage, jalapeño pepper, green onion, and tomato; chili flakes; and Oil-Free Mayonnaise (page 62) diluted with freshly squeezed lime juice for serving

METHOD

In a skillet over high heat, warm the coconut butter. Add the onion and garlic and sauté for 3 minutes. Add the cauliflower, cumin, turmeric, paprika, and cayenne pepper and toss well to ensure even coating. If the mixture looks too dry, add the water, cover, and cook for 7 to 10 minutes, or until the cauliflower has softened. Remove from the heat and season with the salt and black pepper. Transfer to a bowl and set aside to cool slightly.

Add the cilantro and the lime zest and juice. Taste for seasoning and adjust as needed. Serve with the tortillas, avocado, cabbage, jalapeño pepper, green onion, tomato, chili flakes, and diluted oil-free mayonnaise.

FLOUR TORTILLAS

I've found that many common packaged food items are quite simple to make at home. Food corporations profit by using inexpensive and basic ingredients, loading them up with additives to guarantee a longer shelf life, and making them so convenient that people wouldn't consider making the same thing from scratch, like tortillas or flatbreads. However, in many home kitchens around the world, flatbreads are always made by hand. These three-ingredient wonders are the perfect vehicle for salsas, curries, and other dips.

MAKES 8

CHOOSE YOUR FAVORITE COMBINATION

FLOUR (1¼ cups, plus more for rolling out the dough)

Cornmeal

Spelt

Whole wheat

WATER (½ cup)

Filtered water

SEASONING (1 teaspoon)

Salt

METHOD

Place the flour into a bowl and add the water and salt. Using a spoon, stir until well combined.

Turn out the dough onto a clean work surface and knead for 5 minutes, or until the dough is pliable. Return the dough to the bowl, cover with a dish towel, and set aside to rest for 15 to 30 minutes.

Warm a large, dry skillet over medium-high heat.

Sprinkle a thin layer of flour on the work surface. Return the dough to the work surface and divide it into eight equal pieces. Roll out each piece into a 5-inch-wide circle. (You can use an inverted bowl to cut out a perfect circle.) Place the first tortilla on the hot skillet and cook for 30 seconds, or until it begins to bubble up and form a few charred spots. Flip it over and cook for 30 more seconds. Remove from the heat, transfer to a plate, and wrap in a dish towel. Continue with the remaining tortillas until all have been cooked.

Use immediately or store in the freezer for future use.

VARIATION: TORTILLA CHIPS—Prepare the tortilla dough as described above, then cut each 5-inch circle into six triangle-shape wedges. Either fry them in a skillet with a little sunflower seed oil for 2 minutes, or until they get crispy, or bake them at 350°F for 12 to 15 minutes.

SALSA

Enjoy the bounty of summer by snacking on a refreshing spicy dip. I prefer my salsa chunky, but you can always blend it a little for a smoother texture. A combination of sweet and spicy and crisp makes for a very healthy and satisfying snack.

CHOOSE YOUR FAVORITE COMBINATION

BASE (2 cups)

Mangoes
Peaches
Pineapple
Tomatoes

LEAFY GREENS (¼ cup chopped)

Fresh basil
Fresh cilantro
Fresh parsley
Microgreens
Spinach

AROMATICS (1–2 tablespoons)

Fresh chives
Garlic
Green onion
Onion
Shallots

ACIDITY (2 teaspoons)

Apple cider vinegar
Freshly squeezed lemon juice
Freshly squeezed lime juice

OPTIONAL ADDITIONS (½–1 cup)

Avocado
Bell peppers, roasted or raw
Corn (cooked)
Mangoes
Peaches
Pineapple
Radishes
Strawberries

SPICE (to taste)

Cayenne pepper
Chili pepper*
Smoked paprika

*Some chilies are spicier than others. If you want less heat, carefully remove the seeds—and be extra careful when handling them as they can cause a burning sensation on your fingertips.

SUMMER PEACH SALSA

MAKES 2 CUPS

2 peaches, diced
1 cup cooked corn
½ cup chopped roasted red pepper
¼ cup chopped fresh cilantro
1 garlic clove, minced

2 teaspoons freshly squeezed lime juice
½ teaspoon cayenne pepper
½ teaspoon salt, plus more to taste

METHOD

Combine all of the ingredients in a bowl and stir well (you can also pulse this a few times in the food processor if you prefer a smoother salsa). Set aside to allow the flavors to combine for 2 hours. Taste for seasoning and adjust as needed.

Serve or store refrigerated in an airtight container.

RAINBOW ROLLS

This is perhaps the most fun way to enjoy a salad. You'll find that you don't need very much to fill up these rolls, especially if you're using a colorful variety of produce. Not only is eating a spectrum of vibrant vegetables appetizingly cheerful, it also ensures that your body is getting all the right nutrients. Consuming such a variety can strengthen your immune system. Follow the same simple rule you'd follow for any salad, snack, or soup: Make sure all the colors of the rainbow are included for a wholesome, naturally nutritious meal.

CHOOSE YOUR FAVORITE COMBINATION

WRAPS (1 bunch— use large leaves)

Bok choy

Cabbage

Chard

Collard greens

PROTEIN (½ cup)

Hummus (page 98)

Legumes

Spicy Peanut Sauce (page 180)

Tahini

Tofu

FILLINGS (½ cup of each color)

Asparagus, sliced

Avocado, sliced

Beets, julienned

Bell peppers, sliced

Cabbage, shredded

Carrots, sliced

Celery, sliced

Cucumbers, sliced

Green beans, sliced

Green onions, sliced

Mangoes, sliced

Radishes, sliced

Sweet potatoes, sliced (roasted or steamed for 20 minutes)

LEAFY GREENS (2 cups, finely shredded; optional)

Arugula

Bok choy

Fresh herbs

Kale

Lettuce

Microgreens

Radicchio

Spinach

Sprouts (page 24)

DIPPING SAUCE (as needed)

Cashew Cream (page 160)

Garlic Mayonnaise (page 62)

Hoisin Sauce (page 145)

Homemade Harissa (page 126)

Spicy Peanut Sauce (page 180)

METHOD

Prepare all the filling vegetables and shred the leafy greens, if using. Cook the sweet potatoes, if using, and you can sauté or steam the asparagus and green beans for 5 minutes, if desired. Root vegetables can either be julienned or sliced paper-thin with a mandolin; other vegetables should be sliced into long, thin strips.

BOK CHOY RAINBOW ROLLS

1 bunch bok choy

1 carrot, julienned

2 watermelon radishes, julienned

½ cup finely shredded red cabbage

1 avocado, sliced into long strips

1 cup Hummus (page 98)

METHOD

Fill a large bowl with ice water and set aside.

Bring a medium stockpot of water over high heat to a boil.

Separate the leaves of the bok choy from the core. Parboil each leaf by dipping it into the boiling water for 30 seconds, or until softened; then, immediately put it into the ice bath to stop the cooking process. Drain and pat dry with a clean dish cloth.

Using a sharp knife, shave the curved thicker bottom portion of each leaf so it is the same thickness as the stalk and flexible enough to roll up smoothly when filled (they're easier to roll if you use only the dark green, leafy portions).

Spread a tablespoonful of the hummus in the center of each leaf and then arrange the fillings next to each other in a tight line. Don't overstuff them; be sure to leave lots of space around the sides so that the leaves will be easy to roll up. Roll up each one like an open-ended burrito—fold in the bottom and then roll tightly. Repeat until all of the rolls have been filled and wrapped.

Serve.

SPICY PEANUT SAUCE

¾ cup unsalted peanuts

¼ cup filtered water

2 tablespoons pure maple syrup

2 tablespoons low-sodium tamari or soy sauce

1 (½-inch) piece ginger, freshly grated

1 teaspoon apple cider vinegar

1 garlic clove

¼ teaspoon cayenne pepper

METHOD

In a blender or food processor fitted with the "S" blade, combine all of the ingredients and blend until smooth.

DUMPLINGS

It's always a good idea to do a little meal prep when you have the time. I first started making my own dumplings when we were living in Tokyo and I began to miss Chinese dumplings. It's great to have a stash in the freezer for an easy, cozy meal you can heat up quickly. Ready-made wrappers are certainly convenient, but since I've gone plastic-free, I've found that making them from scratch is easy . . . and rather therapeutic. To prevent them from falling apart, make sure the filling isn't too wet. Recipes for traditional dumplings, which are stuffed with meat and leafy greens, often call for you to salt the shredded greens and set them aside to rest for 1 hour so the moisture is drawn out. Then, you rinse off the salt and squeeze out any excess liquid before stuffing. When making vegan dumplings, a mixture of vegetables and tofu, it's easier to sauté everything and cook off the excess moisture.

CHOOSE YOUR FAVORITE COMBINATION

WRAPPERS
(1 portion)

LEAFY GREENS FILLING (2 cups)

Bok choy
Cabbage
Chard
Collard greens
Kale
Watercress

AROMATICS
(2–3 tablespoons)

Fresh chives
Freshly grated ginger
Garlic
Green onion
Leeks
Onion
Shallots

TO COOK THE DUMPLINGS

3 tablespoons sunflower seed oil

+

¼ cup filtered water

OTHER FILLINGS
(2 cups)

Butternut squash
Daikon
Mushrooms
Tofu

SEASONINGS

1 tablespoon low-sodium tamari or soy sauce

+

½ teaspoon salt

+

¼ teaspoon white pepper

+

1½ tablespoons olive oil

NEW YEAR'S DUMPLINGS

MAKES 24

FOR THE WRAPPERS

3 cups white whole wheat flour

1 teaspoon baking powder

¼ teaspoon salt

1 cup hot water

1 tablespoon light sesame oil

FOR THE FILLING

1½ tablespoons olive oil, plus more as needed

2 cups finely chopped fresh spinach

1 cup finely diced butternut squash

6 ounces extra-firm tofu, finely chopped

1 stalk green onion, finely chopped

1 (2-inch) piece ginger, freshly grated

1 tablespoon tamari or soy sauce

½ teaspoon salt

¼ teaspoon white pepper

TO COOK THE DUMPLINGS (PER BATCH)

3 tablespoons sunflower seed oil

¼ cup filtered water per batch

METHOD

Make the wrappers: In a large bowl, sift together the flour, baking powder, and salt. Add the hot water and sesame oil and stir until the mixture begins to clump together. Knead in the bowl until a ball of dough forms.

Turn out the dough onto a clean work surface and knead for 10 more minutes, or until the dough becomes smooth and elastic (like Play Doh). Wrap the dough in parchment paper and set aside to rest at room temperature for 20 minutes, but not for more than 1 hour.

Make the filling: Warm a large, dry skillet over high heat. Add 1½ tablespoons of the olive oil, swirling the skillet to ensure the bottom is well coated. Add the filling ingredients and sauté for 5 to 7 minutes, or until the mixture is softened and any liquid has evaporated.

Transfer to a bowl and set aside to cool for at least 30 minutes, stirring the mixture occasionally to ensure the steam releases.

On a clean, lightly floured work surface, roll the wrapper dough into a long strand about 1-inch in diameter and divide it into 24 equal pieces. Using a rolling pin, flatten each of the pieces and roll them out to ⅛-inch-thick rounds (if desired, trim these to uniform sizes using either a large circular cookie cutter or trace around them with a small inverted bowl and a sharp knife). Cover the rolled-out dough rounds with parchment paper to keep it from drying out.

Have a seat and get comfortable at a clean, dry work surface. Place a little water in a small bowl for sealing the wrappers and line a baking sheet with parchment paper.

Assemble the dumplings: Place one dough round in the palm of your hand. Place one spoonful of the filling in the center of the dough round; take care not to overfill, or

(continued)

they'll be difficult to close. Dip your fingertip into the water and moisten the entire perimeter of the wrapper. Fold the wrapper in half—into a semi-circle—and firmly pinch the edges together to seal (you can then pinch pleats into the folds as well, although that isn't necessary). Place the assembled dumpling onto the prepared baking sheet and continue until you run out of wrappers or filling. (If you plan to cook the dumplings at a later date, at this point, you can place the tray into the freezer. Make sure the dumplings are placed in a single layer. After 3 hours, or when frozen, transfer to a container for future use.)

Warm a large, dry skillet over high heat. Add 1½ tablespoons of the sunflower seed oil, swirling the pan around to ensure even coating of the entire surface. Add some of the dumplings in a single layer, making sure not to overcrowd the pan, and gently shake the pan to ensure that the dumplings get coated with oil and don't stick to the bottom of the pan.

Reduce the heat to medium, cover, and toast for 5 minutes.

Carefully add the ¼ cup of the water to the pan, cover, and cook for 6 minutes, or until steamed through and the liquid has evaporated. Drizzle on 1 more tablespoon of the oil. Cook, uncovered, for 3 more minutes, or until the skin has crisped up. Turn the dumplings over, shaking the pan to keep them from sticking to the bottom, and cook, uncovered, for 3 more minutes, or until crisped on the other side. Add more of the oil between batches to keep the surface well coated.

Serve immediately.

SCALLION GINGER SAUCE

1 (2-inch) piece ginger, finely chopped

1 green onion, finely chopped

1½ teaspoons sesame oil

¼ teaspoon salt

CHILI DIPPING SAUCE

2 small chili peppers, finely sliced

2 tablespoons tamari or soy sauce

1 teaspoon rice vinegar

METHOD

Stir together each of the sauce ingredients into two small bowls.

RATATIAN

Ever since I saw the Pixar movie *Ratatouille*, I knew I had to make ratatouille this way. Traditional ratatouille is a peasant vegetable stew of mushy vegetables, but this preparation method is much more impressive and the vegetables don't all fall to pieces! This is also one of my all-time favorite dishes to prepare with children of any age. I still prefer to call it a ratatouille, but I'm often corrected and told it's either a *tian* or *confit byaldi*. So I came up with my own name for this dish: *Ratatian*. I've tried it with all sorts of sauces as the base, and I'm delighted with the outcome every time! Try to use vegetables that are roughly the same diameter.

CHOOSE YOUR FAVORITE COMBINATION

LIQUID BASE (1 cup)

Cashew Cream (page 160)

Creamy Soup (page 118)

Curry (page 194)

Fresh tomato puree

Raw Marinara Sauce
(page 139)

**AROMATICS
(2–3 tablespoons)**

Fresh chives

Freshly grated ginger

Garlic

Green onion

Leeks

Onion

Shallots

OIL (2 tablespoons)

Coconut

Olive

Sesame, light

Sunflower seed

HERBS (3 teaspoons)

Fresh basil

Fresh oregano

Fresh parsley

Fresh thyme

VEGETABLES (5 pieces)

Beets

Bell peppers

Carrots

Delicata squash

Eggplant

Parsnips

Plum tomatoes

Potatoes

Summer squash

Sunchokes

Sweet potatoes

Turnips

Zucchini

SEASONING (¼ teaspoon)

Freshly ground black
pepper

Salt

RATATOUILLE'S RATATOUILLE

MAKES 6 TO 8 SERVINGS

3 medium tomatoes

1 shallot, chopped

1 garlic clove, chopped

2 tablespoons olive oil

3 teaspoons fresh oregano

Salt, to taste

Freshly ground black pepper,
   to taste

1 Asian eggplant

1 small zucchini

1 small summer squash

½ red bell pepper, deseeded

3 small plum tomatoes

METHOD

Preheat the oven to 400°F.

In a food processor fitted with the "S" blade, process the tomatoes, shallot, and garlic until pureed.

Transfer to a 10-inch round baking dish. Drizzle with 1 tablespoon of the olive oil and sprinkle with ½ of the oregano. Season with the salt and black pepper.

Using a mandolin or a really sharp knife, thinly and evenly slice the eggplant, zucchini, summer squash, and bell pepper into ⅛-inch-thick rounds and strips (the thinner, the better!). Using a sharp knife, slice the plum tomatoes as evenly as possible. Compile the vegetable slices into colorful, patterned mini-stacks.

Arrange these vegetable stacks, a few at a time, into the prepared baking dish in a concentric spiral pattern from the outer edge to the inside, taking care to fan them out a bit. Stuff in as many vegetable slices as possible, saving the smaller rounds for the center of the dish. Drizzle with the remaining 1 tablespoon of the olive oil and season with the salt and black pepper. Sprinkle with the remaining oregano.

Cover the dish with a piece of parchment paper cut to fit just inside the dish's rim, directly atop the arranged vegetables, and bake for 40 minutes to 1 hour, or until softened but not limp, depending on the thickness of your vegetable slices. Remove from the oven.

Serve immediately.

(continued)

Here are some impressive ratatian creations by:

ROW 1: @ikaputri3 @chef_seabones @avivawittenberg
ROW 2: @rainbowplantlife @theradiantkitchen @mangelka
ROW 3: @highonwholesome @urbankitchenapothecary @plasticfreefoodie

More inspiration can be found on Instagram #ratatian

GRATIN

Gratin is a favorite dish at our holiday table, but using traditional cream is too decadent, filling, and over-the-top. I love this vegan variation, as it adds extra protein to a side dish. The vegetables should be thinly sliced; they can be arranged like Ratatian (page 185) or layered evenly on top of each other in a high-rimmed baking dish.

CHOOSE YOUR FAVORITE COMBINATION

VEGETABLES (3 pounds)

Beets	Mushrooms
Butternut squash	Parsnips
Carrot	Potatoes
Cauliflower	Summer squash
Celery root	Sunchokes
Delicata squash	Sweet potatoes
Eggplant	Turnips
	Zucchini

SEASONING

Freshly ground black pepper

Salt

OPTIONAL TOPPING

Fresh herbs

Vegan Parmesan (page 191)

CREAM

2 tablespoons coconut or other vegan butter

+

2 tablespoons arrowroot powder

+

2 cups unsweetened Plant Milk (page 82)

TRI-COLOR GRATIN

MAKES 5 TO 6 SERVINGS

- 2 tablespoons coconut butter
- 2 tablespoons arrowroot powder
- 2 cups unsweetened Almond Milk (page 82)
- 2 beets
- 2 large carrots
- 1 celery root
- Salt to taste
- Freshly ground black pepper to taste
- ½ cup Vegan Parmesan (recipe follows)

METHOD

Preheat the oven to 350°F. Grease a high-rimmed baking dish.

In a small saucepan over medium heat, melt the coconut butter. Stir in the arrowroot powder until a thick paste forms.

(continued)

Reduce the heat to low and add a splash of the almond milk—just enough to dilute the paste and to ensure that there aren't any floury lumps. While stirring constantly, continue to gradually add the milk until it is all in the saucepan.

Raise the heat to medium and cook, stirring occasionally, for 6 to 8 minutes, or until the mixture thickens to the consistency of a thick gravy. Remove from the heat and set aside to cool.

Peel the vegetables, reserving the peels for making Root-to-Leaf Stock (page 215). Using a mandolin or a really sharp knife, thinly and evenly slice the vegetables into ¼-inch-thick slices (the thinner, the better!).

Place the beets in several layers into the prepared baking dish. Season with the salt and black pepper and pour a third of the thickened almond milk over it. Repeat with all the carrots, and then all the celery root slices, pausing between each layer to season and add the rest of the thickened almond milk.

Bake for 1 hour. Remove from the oven.

Raise the heat to 400°F. Sprinkle an even layer of the vegan parmesan on top of the layered vegetables and return to the oven. Bake for 15 more minutes, or until the top is browned. Remove from the oven.

Serve hot.

VEGAN PARMESAN

MAKES ¾ CUP

1 cup raw cashews
¼ cup nutritional yeast

½ teaspoon salt

METHOD

In a blender, combine the ingredients and blend until the mixture has the consistency of coarse sand.

Use or store in an airtight jar in the refrigerator.

STUFFED VEGGIES

Whether you're looking to make an all-in-one weeknight meal or getting ready for a dinner party, preparing the ingredients for this dish and stuffing them in advance makes it easy to pop the whole thing in the oven and quickly heat it through. They're fun to eat, too! If you use seasonal ingredients for the stuffing, along with a variety of pulses, grains, and greens, the possibilities are endless.

CHOOSE YOUR FAVORITE COMBINATION

VEGETABLES TO STUFF

Acorn squash

Bell peppers

Butternut squash

Delicata squash

Eggplant

Mushrooms

Onions

Summer squash

Tomatoes

Zucchini

AROMATICS (1–2 tablespoons)

Fresh chives

Freshly grated ginger

Garlic

Green onion

Leeks

Onion

Shallots

STUFFING

1 cup cooked beans (page 26)

+

1 cup cooked grains

+

1 cup leafy greens

HERBS & SPICES (1–2 teaspoons)

Freshly ground black pepper

Ground cumin

Curry powder

Ground fennel

Fresh oregano

Fresh parsley

Smoked paprika

Fresh rosemary

Fresh sage

Fresh tarragon

Fresh thyme

STUFFED DELICATA SQUASH

MAKES 4 SERVINGS

1 tablespoon olive oil, plus more for coating

1 small onion, finely chopped

½ cup lentils, rinsed

½ cup tri-color quinoa blend, rinsed

1 teaspoon fresh oregano

1 teaspoon fresh basil

1 teaspoon fresh thyme

1 garlic clove, minced

2 cups boiling filtered water

1 cup finely chopped kale, plus more for serving

1 teaspoon salt

2–3 delicata squash, seeds removed and cut into 3-inch segments

Pomegranate arils for garnish

METHOD

Preheat the oven to 400°F. Lightly grease a shallow-rimmed baking dish.

In a medium saucepan over medium-high heat, warm the olive oil. Add the onion and sauté for 3 to 5 minutes, or until softened. Add the lentils, quinoa, herbs, and garlic and toss until evenly coated. Carefully pour in the water and bring the mixture to a boil.

Reduce the heat to low, cover, and simmer for 20 minutes.

Uncover and stir in the 1 cup of kale and the salt. Remove from the heat and set aside to cool.

Tightly pack the lentil-quinoa mixture into the delicata segments and place them into the prepared baking dish. Bake for 30 to 40 minutes. Remove from the oven and set aside to cool for 10 minutes.

Add the remaining kale to the dish and sprinkle with the pomegranate arils. Serve.

CURRY

Curry from any part of the globe is a staple in our household. We all enjoy the warming spices, and—more importantly—I love the anti-inflammatory, immune-boosting benefits of turmeric. Did you know that pairing black pepper with turmeric dramatically increases its bioavailability? Repurpose any leftovers and make them much more flavorful by throwing them into a delicious, piquant curry sauce. Curry sauce and rice was my favorite lunch in my high school's cafeteria, but now I know better, so I make sure to add lots of vegetables and pulses to make it a complete meal. Some Indian restaurants like to make curry sauce on its own and steam the vegetables (recipe follows) separately so the vegetables don't get overcooked and the sauce doesn't get watery.

CHOOSE YOUR FAVORITE COMBINATION

BASE

1 tablespoon olive oil

+

1–2 garlic cloves, chopped

+

1 small onion, chopped

+

1 (½-inch) piece ginger, freshly grated

+

½ teaspoon salt

FLAVOR

Caribbean

Japanese

Thai Green

Tikka Masala (recipes follow)

LIQUID (additional 1–2 cups, to desired consistency)

Coconut Milk (page 82)

Filtered water

Root-to-Leaf Stock (page 215)

PROTEIN (1 cup)

Pulses (cooked; page 26)

Tofu

FINISHING TOUCHES (to taste)

Chili pepper, fresh or dried, to taste

Fresh herbs

Freshly squeezed citrus juice and zest

VEGETABLES (1 pound)

Beans

Broccoli

Brussels sprouts

Carrots

Eggplant

Okra, whole

Pumpkin

Zucchini

+

(in the last minute, 1 cup)

Fresh herbs

Leafy greens, finely shredded

Microgreens

Opposite: Caribbean Peanut Curry, page 198

THAI GREEN CURRY

1 tablespoon olive oil

1 small onion, chopped

1 (½-inch) piece ginger, freshly grated

1–2 garlic cloves, chopped

½ teaspoon salt

¼ cup chopped fresh cilantro

1 stem lemongrass, bottom third only, or 6 full blades of the North American variety

2 kaffir lime or lemon balm leaves

2 teaspoons coriander seeds or ground coriander

½ teaspoon cumin seeds or ground cumin

¼ teaspoon green peppercorns

1 cup Coconut Milk (page 82)

1 cup filtered water or Root-to-Leaf Stock (page 215)

1 pound steamed vegetables of your choice

METHOD

In a large stockpot over high heat, warm the olive oil. Add the onion, ginger, garlic, and salt and sauté for 3 to 5 minutes. Stir in the cilantro, lemongrass, lime leaves, coriander, cumin, and green peppercorns and sauté for 1 to 2 minutes, or until fragrant. Remove from the heat.

Transfer the contents of the saucepan to a blender. Add the coconut milk and blend until smooth.

Return the contents of the blender to the saucepan. Add the vegetables of your choice and as much of the water as needed to just cover the mixture. Place over high heat and bring to a boil.

Reduce the heat to low and simmer for 12 to 17 minutes, or until the vegetables have softened. Remove from the heat.

TIKKA MASALA

1 tablespoon olive oil

1 small onion, chopped

1 (½-inch) piece ginger, freshly grated

1–2 garlic cloves, chopped

½ teaspoon salt

1 tomato, finely chopped

2–4 tablespoons finely chopped fresh cilantro leaves and stems

1 tablespoon paprika

1 teaspoon ground coriander

1 teaspoon garam masala

1 teaspoon ground cumin

1 teaspoon ground turmeric

¼ teaspoon freshly ground black
    pepper

¼ teaspoon ground cardamom

¼ teaspoon cayenne pepper
    (more if you like it spicy!)

1–2 cups filtered water or Root-
    to-Leaf Stock (page 215)

1 pound steamed vegetables of
    your choice

METHOD

In a large stockpot over high heat, warm the olive oil. Add the onion, ginger, garlic, and salt and sauté for 3 to 5 minutes. Stir in the tomato, cilantro, paprika, coriander, garam masala, cumin, turmeric, black pepper, cardamom, and cayenne pepper and sauté for 1 to 2 minutes, or until fragrant. Remove from the heat.

Transfer the contents of the saucepan to a blender. Add ½ cup of the water and blend until smooth.

Return the contents of the blender to the saucepan. Add the vegetables of your choice and as much of the remaining water as needed to just cover the mixture. Place over high heat and bring to a boil.

Reduce the heat to low and simmer for 12 to 17 minutes, or until the vegetables have softened. Remove from the heat.

Transfer to a serving bowl and serve immediately.

JAPANESE CURRY

1 tablespoon olive oil

1 small onion, chopped

1 (½-inch) piece ginger, freshly
    grated

1–2 garlic cloves, chopped

½ teaspoon salt

½ apple, peeled and cored

Handful cherry tomatoes

3 tablespoons flour of your choice

2 teaspoons ground coriander

1 teaspoon ground turmeric

1 teaspoon ground cumin

1 teaspoon garam masala

¼ teaspoon freshly ground black
    pepper

1¼ cups filtered water

2 tablespoons 100-percent cocoa
    or cacao powder

2 tablespoons pure maple syrup

2 tablespoons low-sodium tamari
    or soy sauce

METHOD

In a small saucepan over high heat, warm the olive oil. Add the onion, ginger, garlic, and salt and sauté for 3 to 5 minutes. Add the apple, tomatoes, flour, coriander, turmeric, cumin, and garam masala and sauté for 1 to 2 minutes, or until fragrant. Remove from the heat.

Transfer the contents of the saucepan to a blender. Add the water, cocoa powder, maple syrup, and tamari or soy sauce and blend until smooth.

Return the contents of the blender to the saucepan and place it over medium-high heat. Bring to a boil.

Reduce the heat to low and simmer for 10 to 15 minutes, or until thickened. Remove from the heat.

Transfer to a serving bowl and serve immediately.

CARIBBEAN PEANUT CURRY

MAKES 4 SERVINGS

2 cups filtered water

½ cup unsalted peanuts

1 small onion, chopped

1 jalapeño pepper

1 (½-inch) piece ginger, freshly grated

2 garlic cloves, chopped

1 tablespoon olive oil

2 teaspoons ground turmeric

½ teaspoon cayenne pepper

½ teaspoon salt

¼ teaspoon ground cumin

¼ teaspoon yellow mustard

¼ teaspoon freshly ground black pepper

⅛ teaspoon freshly grated nutmeg

3 tablespoons coconut butter, softened

½ pound okra, whole

2 purple carrots, cut into ½-inch slices

¼ pound broccoli, cut into bite-size pieces

1 cup cooked red kidney beans (page 26)

1 cup microgreens

Freshly squeezed juice of 1 lime

METHOD

In a blender, combine the water, peanuts, onion, jalapeño pepper, ginger, garlic, oil, turmeric, cayenne pepper, cumin, mustard, black pepper, and nutmeg and blend together.

Transfer the contents of the blender to a large saucepan over medium-high heat. Stir in the coconut butter as you bring to a boil.

Reduce the heat to low, cover, and simmer for 10 to 12 minutes. Remove from the heat.

Place a separate pot fitted with a steamer basket and containing 1 inch of water over high heat and bring to a boil. Add the vegetables in batches and steam for 2 to 3 minutes per batch. Remove from the heat and set aside.

Return the sauce to high heat and stir in the vegetables and kidney beans. Cook for 3 minutes, or until heated through. Remove from the heat.

Transfer to a serving bowl and stir in the microgreens. Add the lime juice and serve immediately.

STEAMED VEGETABLES

Steaming vegetables are an ideal way to cook them and still retain all the nutrients. Unless instructed otherwise below, be sure to evenly cut them into bite-size pieces to ensure uniform cooking.

2 TO 3 MINUTES (1 CUP EACH)

Asparagus, trimmed, whole	Green peas, whole
Broccoli, cut into bite-size pieces	Leafy greens, whole
Carrots, ½-inch slices	Okra, whole
Cauliflower, bite-size pieces	Zucchini, ½-inch slices

8 TO 10 MINUTES (1 CUP EACH)

Beets, cut into quarters	Pumpkin, cut in 2-inch chunks
Brussels sprouts, halved	Turnips, cut into 1-inch chunks
Fennel, cut into quarters	Sweet potato, cut into 2-inch chunks
Kohlrabi, cut into eighths	

METHOD

Place a stockpot fitted with a steamer basket and containing 1 inch of water over high heat and bring to a boil. Add the vegetables in batches in a loose layer and steam for the time indicated above per batch. Remove from the heat and repeat as necessary until all vegetables are steamed. Plunge steamed vegetables in an ice bath to prevent them from overcooking. Reheat in sauce when serving.

CHILI

When you're making a vegan chili, loading in a wide variety of vegetables and plenty of warming, spicy flavors means that no one will ever miss the meat. This is a perfect meal for those times when your fridge looks a little empty. You can use up all the bits and bobs of fresh ingredients and make good use of the dry-goods items in your pantry. If you preserve fresh tomatoes or sauce made from them in the freezer, this is the perfect way to enjoy them, too. In late fall, fresh cranberry beans are available at the farmers' market, and I always love to include them in my chili. The bright pink patterns on the shells and beans are really quite beautiful.

CHOOSE YOUR FAVORITE COMBINATION

BEANS (2 cups, fresh or cooked)

Adzuki

Black

Borlotti

Cannellini

Chickpeas

Cranberry

Navy

Pinto

Red kidney

or

(1 cup, dried)

Lentils

LIQUID (2 cups)

Filtered water

Root-to-Leaf Stock (page 215)

TOMATO SAUCE (3 cups/24 ounces)

Raw Marinara Sauce (page 139)

6 tomatoes, blended

HEAT (to taste)

Cayenne pepper

Fresh chili pepper

BASE

1 tablespoon olive oil

+

2 garlic cloves, chopped

+

2 celery stalks, chopped

+

½ onion, chopped

VEGETABLES, ADDITIONAL (2–3 cups)

Acorn squash

Butternut squash

Carrots

Corn

Leeks

Mushrooms

Pumpkin

Sweet potatoes

Zucchini

SPICES

1 teaspoon ground cumin

+

1 teaspoon sweet paprika

+

1 teaspoon dried oregano

PUMPKIN CHILI

MAKES 4 TO 6 SERVINGS

1 tablespoon olive oil

3 carrots, finely diced

2 celery stalks, finely diced

½ onion, finely chopped

2 garlic cloves, minced

2 cups fresh cranberry beans

1 teaspoon ground cumin

1 teaspoon fresh oregano

1 teaspoon sweet paprika

2 cups Raw Marinara Sauce
(page 139)

2 cups filtered water

2 zucchini, finely diced

2 acorn squash, cut in half, seeds
removed, and roasted

¼–½ teaspoon cayenne pepper or
to taste

METHOD

Coat the bottom of a large stockpot with the olive oil and place it over high heat. Add the carrots, celery, onion, and garlic and sauté for 5 minutes, or until the onion is softened.

Stir in the beans, cumin, oregano, and paprika and cook, stirring constantly, for 2 minutes, or until the spices are fragrant. Pour in the raw marinara sauce and the water and bring to a boil.

Reduce the heat to low, cover, and simmer for 40 minutes to 1 hour, or until the beans are soft. About 15 minutes before the cooking time is up, stir in the zucchini.

When the cooking time is complete, stir in the acorn squash and season with the cayenne pepper. Remove from the heat.

Serve hot.

NOTE: If you want to cook the acorn squash along with the rest of the chili rather than roasting it, making it a one-pot meal, just peel and dice it and add it at the same time as the zucchini.

STEW

A one-pot meal is always a win, and it's just as easy to make a lot, so it can last throughout the week. Stews are often more flavorful the next day. Always add a handful or two of dark, leafy greens just before serving to add freshness, as well as nutrients and color. The warming spices in this recipe are good for digestion and circulation—and perfect for the colder months of the year.

CHOOSE YOUR FAVORITE COMBINATION

BASE	SPICES (1 to 3 teaspoons)	VEGETABLES (3–4 cups)	LIQUID (2–3 cups for the stew or ½–1 cup for pie)
2 tablespoons olive oil	Bay leaves	Acorn squash	Filtered water
+	Cayenne pepper	Butternut squash	Root-to-Leaf Stock (page 215)
½ red onion, finely chopped	Dried basil	Carrots	
+	Dried lemongrass	Celery	**LEGUMES (2 cups, fresh or cooked)**
2–3 garlic cloves, finely chopped	Five-spice powder	Celery root	
+	Fresh oregano	Daikon	Adzuki
1 teaspoon salt	Fresh parsley	Fennel	Black
	Fresh rosemary	Green beans	Borlotti
THICKENER (2 tablespoons)	Fresh sage	Kohlrabi	Cannellini
	Fresh tarragon	Leeks	Chickpeas
Brown rice flour	Fresh thyme	Mushrooms	Lentils
Chickpea (gram) flour	Freshly ground black pepper	Okra	Navy
Spelt	Garam masala	Parsnips	Pinto
Whole wheat	Ground cardamom	Peppers	Red kidney
	Ground cinnamon	Potatoes	
	Ground cumin	Pumpkin	
	Ground ginger	Sweet potatoes	
	Ground turmeric	Tomatoes	
	Star anise	Turnips	
	Sweet paprika	Zucchini	

MOROCCAN TAGINE

MAKES 4 SERVINGS

2 tablespoons olive oil

½ red onion, finely chopped

3 garlic cloves, finely chopped

2 tomatoes, chopped

1 tablespoon five-spice powder

1 cinnamon stick or 1 teaspoon ground cinnamon

2 bay leaves

2 tablespoons chickpea (gram) flour

1 sweet potato, cut into 2-inch cubes

1 medium eggplant, cut into 2-inch cubes

1 red bell pepper, seeds removed, cut into 2-inch pieces

2 cups lentils

2–3 cups filtered water

1 teaspoon salt

¼ teaspoon cayenne pepper (optional)

Cooked couscous or rice or Mash (page 204) for serving

METHOD

In a medium stockpot over high heat, warm the olive oil. Add the onion and garlic and gently sauté for 5 minutes, or until soft. Add the chopped tomatoes, chickpea flour, and spices, tossing until well coated. Add the sweet potato, eggplant, and bell pepper and stir well. Add the lentils and water and bring to a boil.

Reduce the heat to low, cover, and simmer for 30 to 40 minutes, or until the eggplant is soft but not mushy. Season with the salt and the cayenne pepper, if using, to taste. Remove from the heat.

Serve hot with the couscous, rice, or mash.

MASH

When it comes to the Thanksgiving meal, for me it's really all about the sides. I was never really a fan of turkey, anyway, and all the side dishes were substantial enough to make a meal. That's how I try to treat every meal, making a variety of vegetables the highlight. Mixing lots of vegetables and proteins with a simple side dish, like mashed potatoes, makes it more nutritionally substantial.

CHOOSE YOUR FAVORITE COMBINATION

VEGETABLES FOR MASH (2–3 pounds)

Butternut squash

Cauliflower

Celery root

Parsnips

Potatoes

Pumpkin

Sunchokes

Sweet potatoes

Turnips

PROTEIN, BEANS (1 cup, cooked)

Cannellini

Chickpeas

Navy beans

PLANT MILK (page 82; 3 tablespoons)

Almond

Brazil nut

Cashew

Coconut

Hazelnut

Hemp

Macadamia

Oat

Pecan

Pepitas (pumpkin seeds)

Pistachio

Sunflower seeds

Walnuts

SPRINKLES (2–3 tablespoons)

Chili flakes

Dukkah

Fresh chives

Freshly ground black pepper

Freshly squeezed lime juice and zest

Green onion

Hemp seeds

Herbs

Nutritional yeast

SALT (½ teaspoon)

CELERY ROOT MASH WITH ROASTED CARROTS

MAKES 4 SERVINGS

4 tablespoons olive oil

1 tablespoon za'atar

1 cup cooked chickpeas (page 26)

2 pounds carrots, scrubbed

4 potatoes, peeled and cubed

1 celery root, peeled and cubed

3 tablespoons Hemp Milk (page 82)

1 garlic clove, minced

¾ teaspoon salt

¼ teaspoon freshly ground black pepper

METHOD

Preheat the oven to 425°F. Line a baking sheet with parchment paper. Mix 2 tablespoons of the olive oil with the za'atar and set aside. Set aside a few spoonfuls of the chickpeas to use as a garnish.

Lightly coat the carrots with the remaining 2 tablespoons of the olive oil and place them on the prepared baking sheet. Roast for 25 minutes. Remove from the oven.

Fill a stockpot half full with water and bring to a boil. Add the potatoes and celery root and boil for 20 minutes, or until soft. Remove from the heat, drain well, and return to the stockpot.

Add most of the chickpeas, the hemp milk, and the garlic to the stockpot and mash well (you can also transfer the mixture to a food processor fitted with the "S" blade and puree the mixture). Season with the salt and black pepper.

Spoon the mixture onto a serving dish. Top with the roasted carrots, the reserved chickpeas, and a drizzle of the za'atar–olive oil mixture.

MARINADES

Simply by combining spices, a kitchen can be transformed into a mode of travel, as you voyage around a world of flavors. Seasoning vegetables makes them flavorful, exciting, and fun. Marinate your veggies for 1 hour at room temperature, or overnight in the refrigerator, before cooking. In these recipes, you'll encounter spice blends that incorporate the six flavors of foods that according to ayurvedic principles all have beneficial effects on the body. Pictured are the Mediterranean, Jerk, and Teriyaki marinades.

MAKES ½ CUP

	CHINESE BBQ	JERK	MEDITERRA-NEAN	MIDDLE EASTERN	TANDOORI	TERIYAKI
SWEET	3 tablespoons Hoisin Sauce (page 145)	1 tablespoon coconut sugar	3 tablespoons olive oil	2 tablespoons allspice + 2 tablespoons olive oil	1 tablespoon olive oil + 1 teaspoon garam masala	1 tablespoon coconut sugar, pure maple syrup, or raw cane sugar
PUNGENT	1 tablespoon paprika	5 garlic cloves, chopped + 1 (2-inch) piece ginger, freshly grated + 1 teaspoon cayenne pepper + 1 teaspoon freshly ground black pepper	4 garlic cloves, chopped	½ red onion, chopped + garlic clove, chopped + ½ teaspoon ground ginger	4 garlic cloves, minced + 2 tablespoons freshly grated ginger + 1 tablespoon sweet paprika + ½ teaspoon cayenne pepper	2 garlic cloves, crushed
BITTER	1 teaspoon powdered ginger	1 tablespoon ground cumin	2 bay leaves	1 tablespoon ground cumin	2 teaspoons ground cumin	1 teaspoon sesame oil
SOUR	1 tablespoon rice vinegar	2 tomatoes + freshly squeezed juice of 1 lime	1 tablespoon freshly squeezed lemon juice	Freshly squeezed juice of ½ lemon	Freshly squeezed juice of 1 lemon or lime	2 teaspoons rice vinegar
ASTRINGENT	1 teaspoon ground coriander	2 tablespoons dried thyme	2 cups chopped fresh thyme, oregano, or parsley	1 teaspoon ground coriander	1 tablespoon ground turmeric	¼ apple, grated
SALTY	3 tablespoons low-sodium tamari or soy sauce	2 teaspoons salt	1 teaspoon salt	1 teaspoon salt	1 teaspoon salt	¼ cup low-sodium tamari or soy sauce

ON THE GRILL

Having a barbecue? There are plenty of meatless options for grilling. Treat vegetables as you would meat and rub them with olive oil, salt, and black pepper . . . but if you want the flavors to really permeate, marinate them overnight or give them a good spice rub. If you aren't able to grill outdoors, then broil them on the high setting placed on a baking sheet with the rack 5 inches or so from the flame (make sure the bamboo sticks are pointing toward the sides of the oven, not the center).

CHOOSE YOUR FAVORITE COMBINATION

VEGETABLES

Asparagus
Beets
Bell peppers
Brussels sprouts
Cabbage
Cauliflower
Corn
Eggplant
Fennel
Garlic scapes
Kale
Kohlrabi
Leeks
Onions
Portobello mushrooms
Summer squash
Sweet potatoes
Zucchini

MARINADES
(see page 208)

Chinese BBQ
Jerk
Mediterranean
Middle Eastern
Tandoori
Teriyaki

or

Olive oil
+
Salt
+
Freshly ground black pepper

VEGETABLE KABOB SALAD

MAKES 4 SERVINGS

1 eggplant, cut into 1-inch cubes
1 summer squash, sliced into 1-inch-thick rounds
1 zucchini, sliced into 1-inch-thick rounds
1 red bell pepper, stemmed and seeded and cut into 2-inch segments
1 orange bell pepper, stemmed and seeded and cut into 2-inch segments

¼ red onion
Freshly squeezed juice of ½ lemon
2 tablespoons olive oil
2 tablespoons allspice
1 tablespoon ground cumin
1 teaspoon ground coriander
1 teaspoon garlic powder
½ teaspoon ground ginger
½ teaspoon salt
2 cups cooked quinoa (page 26) for serving

METHOD

Soak eight bamboo skewers in water for 1 hour.

Preheat the grill to 450°F. Assemble the vegetables on the skewers in layers.

In a small bowl, combine the lemon juice, olive oil, allspice, cumin, coriander, garlic powder, ginger, and salt. Using a pastry brush, apply the mixture to the vegetables.

Place the kebabs on the grill and grill for 15 to 20 minutes, basting and turning them every 5 minutes to ensure even cooking. Remove from the grill.

Serve atop a bed of the quinoa.

ROAST CAULIFLOWER

A whole roasted cauliflower is an impressive vegan main course you can bring to the table triumphantly. Even better, it's incredibly easy to prepare.

CHOOSE YOUR FAVORITE COMBINATION

BASE

Cauliflower (1 whole)

LIQUID (½–1 cup)

Curry (page 194)

Filtered water

Raw Marinara Sauce (page 139)

Root-to-Leaf Stock (page 215)

MARINADES (page 208)

Chinese BBQ

Jerk

Mediterranean

Mexican

Middle Eastern

Tandoori

Teriyaki

WHOLE-ROASTED JERK CAULIFLOWER

MAKES 4 TO 6 SERVINGS

1 large cauliflower

2 tomatoes

5 garlic cloves

Freshly squeezed juice of 1 lime

1 (2-inch) piece ginger, grated

2 tablespoons chopped fresh
  thyme

1 tablespoon coconut sugar

1 tablespoon ground cumin

2 teaspoons salt

1 teaspoon cayenne pepper

1 teaspoon freshly ground black
  pepper

½ cup filtered water

METHOD

Remove the leaves from the cauliflower head and trim off the tough end of the stem. Cut a deep "X" at the base of the stem.

In a blender or food processor fitted with the "S" blade, combine all of the remaining ingredients except the water and blend until smooth.

Gradually rub the tomato mixture onto the cauliflower, making sure to get it into all the crevices. Place it in a large Dutch oven, cover, and refrigerate overnight to marinate.

Preheat the oven to 400°F. Remove the Dutch oven from the refrigerator and add the water. Cover and roast for 1 hour to 80 minutes, or until soft. To crisp up, uncover and broil for another 5 to 7 minutes. Remove from the oven and serve.

ROOT-TO-LEAF VEGGIE STOCK

In this book, we go through a LOT of vegetables, right? Although my recipes strive to use as much of the vegetables as possible, there's still bound to be some scraps. Did you know that there's a lot of nutritional value and flavor in all those bits you often discard? Let's get practical and embrace eating from root to leaf. Save all your soup scraps in a stainless steel box or a large glass jar in the freezer. (Any other scraps should be composted.) When you accumulate a substantial amount—say, about 3 cups—make a nutritious spring soup stock. Onion skins are great for giving the broth a golden caramel color, and mushroom stems lend a rich, earthy flavor. You can use this broth instead of filtered water to add more nutrients to your meals. Following are some bits you can save:

CHOOSE YOUR FAVORITE COMBINATION

SCRAPS (3 cups)

Asparagus ends

Carrot peels and tops

Celery leaves and core

Chard stalks

Corn cobs

Garlic skins

Green bean tips and strings

Herb stems

Kale stalks

Leek greens

Mushroom stems

Onion skins

Pea pod shells

LIQUID

5 cups filtered water

+

1 teaspoon salt

+

1 tablespoon apple cider vinegar

ROOT-TO-LEAF STOCK

MAKES 4 CUPS

5 cups filtered water

3 cups vegetable scraps

1 teaspoon salt

METHOD

Combine all of the ingredients in a medium stockpot over high heat and bring to a boil. Reduce the heat to low, cover, and simmer for 40 minutes to 1 hour. Remove from the heat.

Strain the contents of the stockpot into a glass container and discard any solids. Use immediately, store in the refrigerator in airtight glass jars for up to 5 days, or transfer to Mason jars (leaving 1 inch of airspace in each jar to allow for expansion) and freeze for up to 3 months.

SWEETS

Opposite: Ice Pops, page 222

BLISS BALLS

Bliss balls, a.k.a. *amazeballs*, are my all-time favorite quick, easy energy or protein bites. They are perfect treats—anytime. As with most of my cooking, I like to add vegetables to the mix to provide added texture and nutrition, which makes these sweet treats even more guilt free. Dry-toasting the nuts brings out their flavor; if you plan to use hazelnuts, I recommend removing the bitter skins. You can also use this mixture as a base for Cheesecake (page 244) or even press the mixture into muffin tins to make yummy breakfast tarts filled with Cashewgurt (page 46) and topped with fresh fruit.

CHOOSE YOUR FAVORITE COMBINATION

NUTS or SEEDS (1 cup)	VEGETABLES (¼ cup)	ADDITIONS (½ cup)	TO BIND (2 tablespoons)
Almonds	Avocado	Cashews	Chia seeds
Brazil nuts	Beet	Oats	Flax seeds
Cashews	Carrot	Pepitas (pumpkin seeds)	Nut butter (page 40)
Hazelnuts	Zucchini	Sunflower seeds	
Macadamia nuts			**TO COAT (¼ cup)**
Pecans		**DRIED FRUIT (½ cup/3 ounces)**	Cacao Powder
Pepitas (pumpkin seeds)		Cranberries	Finely ground nuts
Pistachios (shelled)		Dates, pitted	Shredded coconut
Sunflower seeds		Dried figs	
Walnuts		Raisins	

CHOCOLATE HAZELNUT BLISS BALLS

MAKES ABOUT 16 TO 20 BALLS (4 SERVINGS)

1 cup raw hazelnuts

¼ cup old-fashioned rolled oats

¼ cup raw cashews

¼ cup cacao powder

½ avocado

4 dates, pitted (around 3 ounces)

2 tablespoons pure maple syrup

2 tablespoons flax seed meal

METHOD

In a dry skillet over medium heat, toast the hazelnuts for 5 to 10 minutes, until fragrant, shaking the pan often to ensure even toasting. Remove from the heat, immediately transfer to a clean dish towel, and rub the skins off as much as possible.

In a food processor fitted with the "S" blade, process the hazelnuts into a fine meal. Transfer 2 tablespoons of the hazelnut meal to a small bowl for coating the balls and set aside.

Add the oats, cashews, 2 tablespoons of the cacao powder, the avocado, dates, maple syrup, and flax seed meal to the food processor containing the remaining hazelnut flour. Process until smooth (the mixture should hold its shape when pinched between your fingertips, but should not be too wet).

Place the remaining cacao powder in a small bowl.

On a clean work surface, form the mixture into 16 to 20 equal balls. Roll each of the balls in either the remaining cacao powder, the reserved hazelnut meal, or both. Place the coated balls on a baking sheet lined with parchment paper and freeze or refrigerate for at least 20 minutes before serving.

Serve or store in the refrigerator.

RAW CHOCOLATE

All it takes to make delicious chocolate are three ingredients—you can add any dried fruits, nuts, or spices to create your own unique combination. You can also use this mixture to drizzle over Pancakes (page 54), French Toast (page 47), or Whole-Grain Porridge (page 53), or for dipping fruit or Cookies (page 231). Without the extra bits, you can even make your own chocolate chips for topping your Super Smoothies (page 86) or for adding to baked treats.

CHOOSE YOUR FAVORITE COMBINATION

CHOCOLATE BASE

⅓ cup cocoa powder

+

⅓ cup coconut oil, melted

+

3 tablespoons pure maple syrup

TOPPINGS (½ cup)

Almonds

Brazil nuts

Cashews

Hazelnuts

Macadamia nuts

Pecans

Pepitas (pumpkin seeds)

Pistachios (shelled)

Sunflower seeds

Walnuts

EXTRA BITS (3 tablespoons)

Dried cranberries

Coconut flakes

Figs

Goji berries

Raisins

PISTACHIO CHOCOLATE BAR

MAKES ½ CUP

⅓ cup cocoa powder

⅓ cup coconut oil, melted

3 tablespoons warm pure maple syrup

½ cup shelled pistachios

METHOD

In a small bowl, stir together the cocoa powder, coconut oil, and maple syrup until the mixture is smooth and the powder has dissolved.

Evenly spread the mixture into a tray lined with parchment paper. Sprinkle on the pistachios and gently press them down into the mixture. Freeze for at least 1 hour.

Slice and serve. Keep refrigerated.

ICE POPS

Fresh fruit is so sweet that you need not add sugar to make icy treats—in fact, when I make ice pops, I usually add a handful of vegetables to balance out the sweetness. Any Super Smoothie (page 86), Savory Blend (page 94), or Chilled Soup (page 122) also makes a great ice pop! As with smoothies, I recommend that you choose ingredients that are the same color, so your Ice Pops are more visually enticing.

CHOOSE YOUR FAVORITE COMBINATION

FRUIT (4 cups)

Avocado
Bananas
Berries
Cherries, pitted
Coconut
Cranberries
Kiwis
Mangoes
Melons
Peaches
Pineapple
Plums

VEGETABLES (¼–½ cup)

Beets
Carrots
Corn
Peas
Sweet potatoes
Spinach
Summer squash
Zucchini

SWEETNESS, OPTIONAL (1–2 tablespoons)

Brown rice syrup
Dates, pitted
Pure maple syrup

ADDITIONS (2–3 teaspoons)

Chilies
Chia seeds
Citrus zest
Dark chocolate
Fresh herbs
Freshly grated ginger
Nut Butter (page 40)
Nuts

ACIDITY (1 teaspoon; not for creamy pops)

Freshly squeezed lemon juice

Freshly squeezed lime juice

LIQUID (as needed)

Coconut water
Filtered water
Freshly squeezed orange juice
Fruity Water (page 81)
Sun Tea (page 79)

CREAMY

Cashew Cream (page 160)
Plant Milk (page 82)

PIÑA MANGOLADA POPS

MAKES 6

2 cups pineapple chunks
1 mango
½ coconut (meat and water)
½ cup chopped summer squash

1 tablespoon freshly grated ginger
1 teaspoon freshly squeezed lime juice

METHOD

In a blender, combine all the ingredients and blend until smooth.

Transfer the contents of the blender to ice pop molds and freeze for at least 4 hours.

SORBET

I've always thought about the luxury of having an ice cream maker, but NYC living space doesn't allow for too many kitchen gadgets! This sheet-pan method could not be any easier, and it's a refreshing way to enjoy fresh fruit during the hot summer. Although it's not necessary, adding alcohol helps keep the mixture from solidifying.

CHOOSE YOUR FAVORITE COMBINATION

FRUIT #1 (3–4 cups)	FRUIT #2 (¼ cup)	LIQUID (¼–1 cup)	OPTIONAL ALCOHOL (1 tablespoon)
Berries	Berries	Coconut water	Brandy
Cherries, pitted	Cherries, pitted	Filtered water	Vodka
Citrus	Freshly squeezed citrus juice and zest	Fruity Water (page 81)	Whiskey
Cucumber, peeled	Kiwi	Sun Tea (page 79)	
Kiwis	Mango		
Mangoes	Melon	**SWEETNESS (3 tablespoons–¼ cup)**	
Melons	Passionfruit		
Peaches	Peach	Brown rice syrup	
Persimmons	Pineapple	Pure maple syrup	
Pineapple		Raw cane sugar	

BLACKBERRY LEMON SORBET

MAKES 4 SERVINGS

3 cups blackberries

¼ cup freshly squeezed lemon juice and grated zest

1 cup filtered water

2–3 tablespoons pure maple syrup

1 tablespoon vodka (optional)

METHOD

Freeze the blackberries overnight.

In a blender, combine all the ingredients and blend until smooth. Strain the contents of the blender through a fine-mesh sieve into a parchment paper–lined loaf or sheet pan.

Freeze for at least 4 hours.

When ready to eat, break into shards, return to the blender and process again. Serve.

NICE CREAM

Store-bought ice cream is way too sweet for me, and I've never found a vegan ice cream that I enjoyed. Making your own Nice Cream is a really easy way to make a healthy, yet decadent, treat. The all-natural, sugar-free goodness of the ingredients in this recipe makes it perfectly acceptable to have ice cream for breakfast, too.

CHOOSE YOUR FAVORITE COMBINATION

BASE (1 cup)

Cashews, soaked overnight and drained

Frozen bananas

Mangoes

SWEETENER (½ cup)

Brown rice syrup

Dates, pitted

Pure maple syrup

Raw cane sugar

FRUIT FLAVORS (1 cup; frozen or fresh)

Avocados

Berries

Cherries, pitted

Kiwis

Mangoes

Peaches

Pineapple

LIQUID (3 tablespoons, or more if necessary)

Coconut Milk (page 82)

Filtered water

Nut Milk (page 82)

OPTIONAL ADDITIONS (¼ cup)

Cocoa powder

Coconut butter

Coconut oil

or

(1 teaspoon)

Ground cinnamon

Vanilla extract

FUN STUFF (½ cup)

Mint leaves

Nut Butter (page 40)

Nuts

Raw chocolate

BUTTER PECAN NICE CREAM

MAKES 4 SERVINGS

1 cup cashews, soaked for 3 hours or overnight and drained

½ cup chopped pecans

¼ cup pitted dates, soaked and drained

¼ cup room-temperature pure maple syrup

¼ cup coconut oil, melted

¼ cup warm filtered water

1 teaspoon vanilla extract

METHOD

In a food processor fitted with the "S" blade, combine all of the ingredients and blend until smooth and creamy, scraping down the sides if necessary.

Spread the mixture into a loaf pan and freeze for 2 hours.

To serve, warm up an ice cream scoop by placing it in a mug of boiled water. Scoop and serve.

PROTEIN-PACKED BROWNIES

Using whole beans instead of flour when baking is a fun way to get your protein in a nutritionally satisfying sweet treat. Chickpeas provide a wholesome texture, making these brownies moist and gooey when "raw," and more like a grain when baked.

CHOOSE YOUR FAVORITE COMBINATION

TO BIND	BASE (15 ounces, cooked)	FAT (¼ cup)	EXTRACT (1 teaspoon)
2 tablespoons flax seed meal + 6 tablespoons filtered water	Black beans	Avocado	Orange
	Chickpeas	Coconut oil	Peppermint
	Lentils	Nut Butter (page 40)	Vanilla
2 tablespoons chia seeds + 6 tablespoons filtered water	+	Tahini	or
	½ teaspoon baking soda		(½ teaspoon)
¼ cup pumpkin	+	**SWEETNESS (½ cup)**	Almond
¼ cup sweet potato	½ teaspoon baking powder	Brown rice syrup	**EXTRA BITS (½ cup)**
	+	Coconut sugar	Chopped nuts
	¼ cup cocoa powder	Pitted dates	Cacao nibs
		Pure maple syrup	Raw chocolate chips
		Raw cane sugar	

CHICKPEA BROWNIES

MAKES 1 (8-INCH SQUARE) TRAY

2 tablespoons flax seed meal

6 tablespoons filtered water

15 ounces cooked chickpeas (page 26)

¼ cup cocoa powder

¼ cup tahini

¼ cup coconut sugar

¼ cup pure maple syrup

1 teaspoon vanilla extract

½ teaspoon baking soda

½ teaspoon baking powder

½ cup chopped walnuts

METHOD

Line an 8-inch square baking dish or loaf pan with parchment paper. If you plan to bake the brownies, preheat the oven to 400°F.

In a small bowl, stir together the flax seed meal and water and let set for 10 minutes.

Transfer the flax mixture to a food processor fitted with the "S" blade. Add all of the remaining ingredients except the walnuts and process into a smooth batter.

Stir about ¾ of the chopped walnuts into the batter, reserving the rest for sprinkling on top, and pour the batter into the prepared pan. Sprinkle the reserved walnuts on top.

If baking, bake for 30 minutes. Remove from the oven and set aside to cool for 15 minutes.

If you do not plan to bake the brownies, freeze for 3 hours or overnight. Transfer to the refrigerator until ready to serve.

Slice and serve.

COOKIES

I must admit that I have a soft spot for cookies. It's probably that satisfying crunch factor. For years, I would bake white-sugar and white-flour holiday cookies for the entire month of December—obviously, not my healthiest time of the year! Over the years, thanks to school bake sales and favorite vegan teachers, I've adjusted my baking to incorporate cleaner ingredients and a combination of wholesome flours, yet still I'm able to completely satisfy that need for cookie comfort.

CHOOSE YOUR FAVORITE COMBINATION

TO BIND

2 tablespoons flax seed meal + 6 tablespoons filtered water

2 tablespoons chia seeds + 6 tablespoons filtered water

½ cup Plant Milk (page 82)

6 tablespoons Aquafaba (page 27)

FAT (9 tablespoons)

Avocado

Coconut butter

Nut Butter (page 40)

Tahini

or

(12 tablespoons)

Coconut oil

Vegan butter

FLAVOR (1 teaspoon)

Ground cardamom

Ground cinnamon

Ground ginger

Lemon

Orange zest

Pumpkin pie spice

Vanilla extract

or

Cocoa powder (replace ⅓ cup of flour)

FLOUR (3 cups for cut-out cookies, mix)

Almond (page 83)

Chickpea (gram)

Finely ground cornmeal

Oat (page 83)

Spelt

Whole wheat

+

1 teaspoon baking soda

+

1 teaspoon salt, optional

OPTIONAL EXTRA BITS (½ cup)

Cacao nibs

Chia Jam (page 42) for thumbprint cookies

Chopped nuts

Dried fruit

Raw chocolate chips

Seeds

(NOTE: If using gluten-free flours, add 1 tablespoon of psyllium husk.)

SWEETENER (1 cup)

Coconut sugar

Raw cane sugar

AVOCOCOA COOKIES

6 tablespoons filtered water

2 tablespoons chia seeds

1 avocado, mashed

1 cup coconut sugar

1 teaspoon vanilla extract

1 cup spelt flour

1 cup chickpea (gram) flour

½ cup Almond Flour (page 83)

½ cup cocoa powder

1 teaspoon baking soda

1 teaspoon salt (optional)

METHOD

In a small bowl, stir together the water and chia seeds. Set aside.

In a large bowl, combine the avocado and coconut sugar. Using a hand mixer or a stand mixer fitted with the paddle attachment, beat on medium speed until well combined. Add in the chia seed–water mixture and the vanilla and beat again until combined. Add the flours, the cocoa powder, the baking soda, and the salt, if using, and beat until a smooth dough forms.

With this dough, you can:

1. Form it into two or three logs, wrap them up in parchment paper, and freeze so they are ready to slice and bake any time.

2. Form it into walnut-size balls, slightly flatten them, and sprinkle them with raw cane sugar.

3. Form it into walnut-size balls, indent each using a ¼ teaspoon measure, and fill the indentation with chia jam.

4. Form it into a ball, wrap it in parchment or wax paper, and refrigerate for 1 hour. Then, on a clean, floured work surface, roll it out to a ¼-inch thickness and cut with cookie cutters. Gather any scraps and re-roll out the dough. Continue until all the dough has been used.

Preheat the oven to 350°F. Line two baking sheets with parchment paper.

Transfer the cookies to the prepared baking sheets and bake for 12 to 18 minutes (depending on the size of the cookies), swapping the top and bottom baking sheets after 6 minutes (bake for a shorter time if you prefer your cookies chewy, and longer if you prefer crisp ones).

TO DECORATE WITH RAW CHOCOLATE: After baking, drizzle or dip half of each cookie into the raw chocolate and place on a cooling rack to harden. If you're in a hurry, stick the dipped cookies in the freezer for 10 minutes to set the chocolate.

CRUMBLE OR GALETTE

Both of these rustic baked treats are perfect, no-fuss vehicles for enjoying a bounty of in-season produce. I've made them both when staying with friends in the countryside—even in kitchens without any special tools, once using a drinking glass as a rolling pin. If you have a food processor, making these pastries can be pretty quick, but there is something comforting about creating a dish without the use of machinery.

CHOOSE YOUR FAVORITE COMBINATION

PASTRY
(1 portion)

Crumble
(recipe follows)

Galette pastry
(recipe follows)

FILLING
(2½–3 cups)

Apples

Blueberries

Butternut squash

Cherries

Cranberries

Figs

Peaches

Pears

Plums

Strawberries

Sweet potatoes

ADDITIONS
(½–1 cup)

Apples

Blueberries

Butternut squash

Cashew Cream
(page 160)

Cherries

Chocolate

Cranberries

Figs

Peaches

Pears

Plums

Strawberries

Sweet potatoes

SWEETENER
(2 tablespoons)

Brown rice syrup

Coconut sugar

Pure maple syrup

Raw cane sugar

FLAVORS
(1–3 teaspoons)

Fresh rosemary

Ground cinnamon

Ground ginger

Lemon zest

Orange zest

FLOUR
(1–2 tablespoons)

Chickpea (gram)

Oat

Spelt

Whole wheat

RUSTIC SUMMER BERRY GALETTE

MAKES 6 TO 8 SERVINGS

FOR THE GALETTE PASTRY

1 cup spelt flour, plus more for
  rolling
½ cup chickpea (gram) flour
2 tablespoons raw cane sugar

¼ teaspoon salt
8 tablespoons very cold vegan
  butter, cut into ¼-inch cubes
3 tablespoons ice-cold water

FOR THE FILLING

2 cups strawberries
1 cup blueberries
2 tablespoons coconut sugar
1 tablespoon freshly squeezed
  lemon juice

1 tablespoon brown rice flour
1 cup sweet Cashew Cream (page
  160)

METHOD

Preheat the oven to 375°F. Line a baking sheet with parchment paper.

Make the galette pastry: In a large bowl, sift together the 1 cup of spelt flour, the chickpea flour, sugar, and salt. Grate the vegan butter into the flour mixture, stirring often so it doesn't get lumpy. Using your fingertips, break down any large lumps so the mixture becomes grainy, like coarse sand. Using a fork, mix in the ice-cold filtered water, 1 tablespoon at a time, until the mixture just comes together. Form the dough into one large ball.

Sprinkle some of the spelt flour on a piece of parchment paper as well as on a rolling pin. Roll out the dough into a circle about ¼-inch thick.

Place the dough circle or circles on the prepared baking sheet.

Make the filling: In a large bowl, toss the filling ingredients together.

Spread the cashew cream in a large circle in the center of the rolled-out dough, leaving a 2-inch space around the edges for folding over and framing the filling.

Place the berry filling on top of the cashew cream. Fold the pastry edges over, overlapping the outer edges of the berry filling and framing it so the juices do not run out during baking. Pinch each fold together.

Bake for 30 to 35 minutes. Remove from the oven and serve warm.

PLUM CRUMBLE

FOR THE TOPPING

¼ cup chickpea (gram) flour

3 tablespoons raw cane sugar

4 tablespoons very cold vegan
   butter, cut into ¼-inch cubes,
   plus more for greasing

¼ cup old-fashioned rolled oats

¼ cup chopped pecans

1 teaspoon baking powder

¼ teaspoon salt

FOR THE FRUIT FILLING

1 tablespoon vegan butter

8 plums, pitted and diced

1 apple, peeled and diced

2 tablespoons brown rice flour

2 tablespoons raw cane sugar

1 teaspoon freshly grated ginger

METHOD

Preheat the oven to 375°F.

Make the topping: In a large bowl, sift together the flour and the sugar. Grate the 4 tablespoons of the vegan butter into the flour mixture, stirring often so it doesn't get lumpy. Add the remaining topping ingredients. Using your fingertips, combine the mixture. Set aside.

Generously grease a small, deep baking dish with the butter.

Make the filling: In a large bowl, toss together the fruit pieces, flour, sugar, and ginger until evenly coated. Pour into the prepared baking dish.

Sprinkle the topping in an even layer on top of the filling. Bake for 25 to 35 minutes, or until the top is golden and crisp. Remove from the oven and serve warm.

SHORTCAKE

I had to include this classic sweet treat because strawberry shortcake is a regular birthday request in my family. It's also a treat they anticipate whenever we go strawberry picking in the summer. This recipe, which uses minimal sugar, also reminds me of traditional English teatime. When you need a replacement for whipped cream, aquafaba really is magic.

CHOOSE YOUR FAVORITE COMBINATION

FLOUR (2½ cups)

Buckwheat

Chickpea (gram)

Oat

Spelt

Whole wheat

+

(1 tablespoon)

Baking powder

SWEET (5 tablespoons)

Coconut sugar

Raw cane sugar

OIL (8 tablespoons)

Coconut

Vegan butter

TO BIND

1 tablespoon flax seed meal + 3 tablespoons filtered water

1 tablespoon chia seeds + 3 tablespoons filtered water

¼ cup ripe banana, mashed

¼ cup grated apple

4 tablespoons Aquafaba (page 27)

¼ cup sweet potato or pumpkin puree

LIQUID (½ cup)

Plant Milk (page 82)

FILLING (1½–2 cups)

Blackberries

Blueberries

Cherries

Mangoes

Peaches

Persimmons

Strawberries

+

1 tablespoon pure maple syrup

RASPBERRY SHORTCAKE WITH AQUAFABA WHIPPED CREAM

MAKES 8 TO 10 SERVINGS

FOR THE CAKES

2 cups white whole wheat flour

½ cup spelt flour

5 tablespoons raw cane sugar

1 tablespoon baking powder

8 tablespoons cold vegan butter

½ cup Coconut Milk (page 82)

4 tablespoons Aquafaba (page 27)

FOR THE FILLING

1½ cups fresh raspberries

1 tablespoon pure maple syrup

(continued)

½ cup Aquafaba (page 27)

½ teaspoon arrowroot powder

2 tablespoons raw cane sugar

½ teaspoon vanilla extract

METHOD

Preheat the oven to 450°F. Line a baking sheet with parchment paper.

Make the cakes: In a large bowl, sift together the flours, half of the sugar, and the baking powder. Grate the vegan butter into the flour mixture, stirring often with a fork so it doesn't get lumpy. Using your fingertips, break down any large lumps so the mixture becomes fine, even, and crumbly.

In a separate bowl, whisk together the coconut milk and 3 tablespoons of the aquafaba. Gradually pour half of this wet mixture into the dry mixture, using a fork to combine. Continue to add this wet mixture slowly, making sure you add just enough that the dough comes together in a big lump (you may not need all of it).

Sprinkle some of the spelt flour on a piece of parchment paper as well as on a rolling pin. Roll out the dough into one large disc about ¼ inch thick.

Turn out the dough onto a clean, well-floured work surface and roll it out to a ¾-inch thickness. Using the rim of a drinking glass or a 2½-inch cookie cutter, cut out as many rounds as you can. Gather any scraps and re-roll out the dough. Continue until all the dough has been used (you may have to shape the last one by hand).

Place the cakes onto the prepared baking sheet, with each round set about 1 inch apart. Brush the tops with the remaining aquafaba and, using your fingertips, evenly sprinkle the remaining sugar on top of the rounds. Bake for 10 to 15 minutes until golden. Remove from the oven and set aside to cool on a wire rack.

Make the filling: In a small bowl, combine the raspberries and maple syrup and mash them together. Set aside.

Make the whipped cream (best when served immediately): Using a hand mixer or a stand mixer fitted with the whisk attachment, beat the aquafaba on high speed for 10 minutes or until firm, white peaks form. While the mixer continues to run, gradually add the sugar, arrowroot powder, and vanilla.

Slice each cake in half horizontally. Place a spoonful of the filling and a dollop of the whipped cream on each cake half. You can enjoy this open-faced halves or sandwich style.

CAKE

One of my all-time favorite desserts, Sticky Toffee Pudding makes a regular appearance on my holiday table. I've "cleaned up" the traditional recipe by incorporating healthier ingredients and dropping the dairy and eggs. Using almond and chickpea flours makes a denser cake that's also gluten-free and Paleo, but no matter what flours you use, this treat is best served warm.

CHOOSE YOUR FAVORITE COMBINATION

BASE

1 cup (6 ounces) chopped pitted dates

+

1¼ cups filtered water

+

1 teaspoon baking soda

TO BIND

2 tablespoons flax seed meal + 6 tablespoons filtered water

2 tablespoons chia seeds + 6 tablespoons filtered water

½ cup ripe banana, mashed

½ cup freshly grated apple

½ cup sweet potato or pumpkin puree

6 tablespoons Aquafaba (page 27)

OIL (¼ cup)

Coconut

Sunflower seed

Vegan butter

+

(¼ cup)

Nut Milk (page 82)

SWEET (¼ cup)

Coconut sugar

Raw cane sugar

ADDITIONS

1 teaspoon vanilla extract

+

1 teaspoon baking powder

FLOUR (1½ cups)

Buckwheat

Chickpea (gram)

Nut (page 83)

Oat

Spelt

Whole wheat

+

(2 teaspoons)

Baking powder

STICKY TOFFEE PUDDING

MAKES 6 SERVINGS

FOR THE PUDDING

1¼ cups + 6 tablespoons filtered water

2 tablespoons flax seeds

1 cup chopped, pitted dates

1 teaspoon baking soda

¼ cup coconut butter, softened, plus more for greasing

¼ cup coconut sugar

1 teaspoon vanilla extract

1 teaspoon baking powder

1 cup Almond Flour (page 83)

½ cup chickpea (gram) flour

(continued)

½ cup raw cashews, soaked for 3 hours to overnight and drained

5 dates, pitted, chopped, soaked for 3 hours to overnight, and drained

½ cup filtered water

¼ cup pure maple syrup

½ teaspoon vanilla extract

3 tablespoons coconut oil

METHOD

Preheat the oven to 425°F.

Make the pudding: In a small bowl, stir together the 6 tablespoons of the water and the flax seeds. Set aside.

In a small saucepan over medium-high heat, combine the remaining water, the chopped dates, and the baking soda and bring to a boil. Remove from the heat and set aside to cool slightly.

In a large bowl, combine the contents of the saucepan, the ¼ cup of coconut butter, the coconut sugar, the flax seed mixture, and the vanilla. Using a hand mixer or a stand mixer fitted with the paddle attachment, beat on medium speed until well combined. Add the flours and beat until a smooth batter forms.

With the remaining coconut butter, grease a high-rimmed baking dish. Pour the batter into the baking dish until it is ¾ of the way full.

Bake for 40 to 50 minutes. Insert a toothpick into the cake to test for doneness; if it comes out clean, it's ready. If not, bake for 5 more minutes. Remove from the oven and set aside to cool for 20 minutes.

Turn the cake out into a serving bowl.

Make the toffee sauce: In a blender, combine the cashews, dates, water, maple syrup, and vanilla and blend until smooth.

Transfer the contents of the blender to a small saucepan over low heat. Add the coconut oil and stir until the oil melts. Remove from the heat.

Drizzle most of the warm toffee sauce over the cake; reserve some to serve on the side, so everyone can help themselves to more delicious drizzle.

CHEESECAKE

When I was a teenager, we always had a homemade London-style cheesecake in the fridge. I love this more versatile dairy-free version. Although it's small in size, it's just as rich and decadent.

CHOOSE YOUR FAVORITE COMBINATION

CRUST

½ cup nuts of your choice

+

1–2 dates, pitted

+

1 teaspoon chia seeds

SWEETENER (3 tablespoons)

Brown rice syrup

Pure maple syrup

BASE (1½ cup)

Cashews

Macadamia nuts

+

½ teaspoon vanilla extract

+

1 teaspoon freshly squeezed lemon juice

FAT (3 tablespoons)

Coconut butter

Coconut oil

FLAVORS (1 cup)

Bananas

Blueberries

Chocolate

Mangoes

Pineapple

Pumpkin

Raspberries

or

Freshly grated zest of 1 lemon

Freshly squeezed juice of 1 lemon

EXTRA FLAVORS (2 teaspoons)

Freshly grated ginger

Freshly squeezed citrus juice and zest

Ground cinnamon

Mint

Pumpkin pie spice

Vanilla extract

MEYER LEMON AND GINGER CHEESECAKE

MAKES 6 SERVINGS

FOR THE CRUST

½ cup raw almonds

1 date, pitted

1 teaspoon chia seeds

FOR THE CHEESECAKE

1½ cups macadamia nuts, soaked for 8 hours overnight and drained

Freshly squeezed juice and grated zest of 1 Meyer lemon

3 tablespoons brown rice syrup

3 tablespoons coconut oil, melted

2 teaspoons grated ginger

½ teaspoon vanilla extract

Sliced fresh fruit for serving

Fresh lemon slices, thyme leaves, and freshly grated ginger for garnish

(continued)

METHOD

Make the crust: In a food processor fitted with the "S" blade, combine all of the crust ingredients and process for 2 to 3 minutes (the mixture should hold together when you pinch it slightly). Press the mixture into a 5-inch springform pan.

Make the cheesecake: In a food processor fitted with the "S" blade, combine all of the cheesecake ingredients and process until the mixture is smooth. Pour the filling on top of the crust and freeze for at least 4 hours.

Remove the cheesecake from the freezer and set aside to thaw for 5 minutes. Then remove the cheesecake from the springform pan and set aside for 10 minutes.

Slice and serve with the fresh fruit and garnished with the lemon slices, thyme leaves, and grated ginger.

ACKNOWLEDGMENTS

When I was a child, I was usually greeted by my grandmother with, "Have you eaten yet?" As a devout Buddhist, she was vegan, but she still cooked meat for her family. Her kitchen was also filled with washed plastic bags that were hanging up to dry and reuse. I didn't understand her very much as a teenager, but now, I find that I'm a lot like her—although now I tend to just skip the plastic bags altogether.

The concept and format of this book has been years in the making. My food journey has been a very organic one, and my thanks go to the many people who helped create it.

I thank my family for their incredible support and patience, and for venturing to eat all the variations on my attempts to create healthier alternatives for traditional favorites. I'm also grateful for them for adjusting our habits to incorporate a plastic-free, food waste-free life. I am particularly proud of my daughter (Instagram: @skyceramics), who made many of the ceramic pieces featured in this book—thank you for making my food look even better!

Thank you to my incredible sister Monica, who is always there for me, and who always takes the best photos—especially of a certain someone who would much rather be behind the camera than in front of it!

I thank my mom, whose recipes I remember loving throughout my childhood.

Thanks to my dad, who I love for his carefree but solid demeanor, and his "lazy" cooking, which I try to emulate while using whole ingredients.

I can't even begin to express the gratitude I have to the über-talented Michael Ward for the beauty captured in all your beautiful illustrations. Thank you for sharing this journey with me, for all these years.

I want to thank Suran Song for that lightbulb moment of comparing my food philosophy to the practice of yoga, which led to the creation of Yommme and variable food vinyasas.

Brendan Davis at Good Water Farms, thank you for the delicious microgreens I replanted that continue year after year.

Thank you to the team at Florim Ceramiche for providing the beautiful Italian ceramic backdrops that frame my foods so beautifully in these pages.

I thank Nathalie at Global Table Soho, whose wonderful collection of tableware is always a joy to use.

Thank you to my agent Leigh Eisenman, for believing in me, for your infectious enthusiasm, and constant support.

I thank my good friends and family, who always are happy to let me descend upon their kitchens loaded with veggies.

I send a big thanks to Róisín Cameron and the team at The Countryman Press, for making my book become a reality.

The wonderful Instagram food community is a constant source of inspiration, personal growth, and support. My thanks goes to all the "foodstagrammers" who shared their beautiful images with me for the #plasticfreefoodie eMagazine, as well as for this book through my Instagram hashtag parties: Joscelyn Abreu, Mireille Azar, Susanna Bingemer, Kerstin Brachvogel, Nate Burrows, Kimberly Espinel, Verena Frei, Gudrun Gerzabek, Amisha Gurbani, Olena Hassell, Jutri Herman, Jessica Hoffman, Zuliya Khawaja, Meera Nalavadi, Ika Putri Novitawati, Nancy Partington, Sebastian Perez, Sara Kiyo Popowa, Monisha Sharma, Sheil Shukla, Reethika Singh, Rachel Steenland, Didi van Haren, Nisha Vora, Aviva Wittenberg, and Dora Xindaras. My mission has always been to share recipes to encourage people to cook and have fun in the kitchen. I thank my clients, workshop attendees, friends, and anyone else who has tried my recipes; to my friends who let me descend upon their kitchens loaded with veggies; and I thank you, reader, for purchasing this book!

Last, but most certainly not least, I thank the Plastic Ocean Foundation for making the documentary *A Plastic Ocean*, which woke me up to the threat of plastics and empowered me to rethink plastic. This has really been a fulfilling aspect that completes the consciousness that embodies the Yommme food and philosophy. I am eternally thankful for the opportunity to be able to inspire others.

INDEX

Note: Page references in *italics* indicate photographs.